THE GOLF BAG BUDDY

THE GOLF BAG BUDDY

Bill Elliott

D&C
David and Charles

This book is dedicated to everyone who has ever said,
"Golf is not a fair game." And specifically to Val,
Simon, and James, who say it a lot.

A DAVID & CHARLES BOOK
Copyright © David & Charles Limited 2005

David & Charles is an F+W Publications Inc. company
4700 East Galbraith Road
Cincinnati, OH 45236

First published in the US in 2005

Text copyright © Bill Elliott 2005

Bill Elliott has asserted his right to be identified as author of this work
in accordance with the Copyright, Designs and Patents Act, 1988.

A catalogue record for this book is available from the British Library.

ISBN 0 7153 2206 0

Printed in SNP Leefung by China
for David & Charles
Brunel House   Newton Abbot   Devon

Visit our website at www.davidandcharles.co.uk

David & Charles books are available from all good bookshops;
alternatively you can contact our Orderline on (0)1626 334555
or write to us at FREEPOST EX2 110, David & Charles Direct,
Newton Abbot, TQ12 4ZZ (no stamp required UK mainland).
US customers call 800-289-0963 and Canadian customers
call 800-840-5220.

CONTENTS

INTRODUCTION

SAM SNEAD was many things. A champion golfer obviously—Snead won three PGA Championship titles, three Masters Tournaments and The British Open at St. Andrews in 1946—this son of the Virginia backwoods was also something else. He was a wise man. How wise? Well, he once advised a pupil who was struggling to master the intricacies of playing golf even half competently to "cut back on playing for the next month and then give the game up completely."

Years later he told a rookie professional who had asked for a piece of Sam's vast experience to take out with him on the PGA Tour, "If at any moment in any round of golf that you are now going to play you are not thinking of some woman then basically, son, you're wasting your time on this planet." This rookie pro was, I believe, Lee Janzen, who went on to win the 1993 and 1998 U.S. Opens. Janzen, perhaps wisely, never has told us what he was thinking about at the time. Whatever, or whoever, it was, however, it clearly worked.

So what has Sam Snead got to do with this book? Well, probably more than any other golfer before or since, Slammin' Sam embodies much of what is great about this most perverse of games. His talent was beyond debate, but it was his determination to enjoy himself while playing the game on the highest possible plateau that really marks him out. Golf, after all, is the most perverse of sports, a game so contrary that it can drive a man or woman to distraction. No one, not Snead, not Jack Nicklaus, not Tiger Woods, has yet mastered golf completely. Each has had his moments, each has shown what is possible, but the game always wins, reminding even the most obsessive talent that golf is, as Northern Ireland's David Feherty once observed, "a ragged-arsed clown forever dancing on a distant horizon."

The fact that you are reading this suggests that you, like me and like the 60 million other golfers who regularly play the grand old game, are enjoying chasing this ragged-arsed clown. We will never catch him. And nor should we. Golf as a metaphor for life itself is as damn near perfect as it gets inasmuch as it is the journey that is important and not the destination. Snead knew this as well as anyone ever has, and so if *The Golf Bag Buddy* has any patron player in mind, then Sam is as good as, probably better than, any other. What he tried to do throughout his life was to get others to enjoy the game, to savor its almost endless possibilities for fun and eccentricity.

Here, after all, is a game like no other. Even the most accomplished player may find his round shredded by the discovery of an indiscriminate divot or a sudden and unexpected gust of wind. On the other hand, a high handicap hacker may top his shot at a difficult par 3, only to watch with delight as his ball smacks this and that as it meanders toward the green where it drops into the hole. There is no justice in golf and, though diligent practice brings some kind of reward for those who can be bothered with that sort of thing, the majority of us just enjoy playing and accept that, while a career shot may bounce into the rough, a mis-hit one may ricochet into the hole. What we cannot be bothered about is any real understanding of the rules. A smattering, yes. But the whole rigmarole? Rarely. In no other game is this true. And it was from this standpoint that the idea for this book arose.

I have played and written about golf almost all my adult life, and during this time I have constantly been amazed at players' ignorance of the rules in almost any given situation. Frequently this ignorance has been my own. It should not be like this of course. The two world bodies who regulate the game and who are responsible for the rules we all play under, the Royal & Ancient Golf Club of St. Andrews and the United States Golf Association, do their utmost to educate and enrich the lives of every single golfer.

The *Rules of Golf* book they revise and publish every four years is a testimony to their determination to keep the game on an even keel and to reflect the times in which we live. This is the upside. The downside is that, for many, this book carries with it all the attraction of settling down with a railroad timetable for a bit of light reading before turning out the light. To be fair, it is wonderfully precise because it has to be, but it is precise in the manner of a legal document. This is a work best absorbed by a lawyer's mind. My reflections on these rules and what they mean to an average golfer like myself is an attempt to make them more accessible, and I am grateful to an old friend, John Paramor (Chief Referee of the European Tour and the wisest rules guru I know), for casting an expert eye over what I've written. The official Rule Book still, well, rules—but hopefully, by reading this interpretation, you will be better informed next time you go out to play. And this could well be to your advantage, because often ignorance of the rules means that players do not take the relief to which they are entitled.

But there is another reason why I have written this book. Although there are times when golf does not need to be played strictly according to the rules, it is a game that, ultimately, is improved by a knowledge of, and adherence to, these rules. Take on board what I have written and, I promise, you will be better armed to play golf than the great majority. The overriding idea, however, is that we should all enjoy ourselves, and so I have also written about some of the competitions and other games you may play. Some of these are played under the rules, others are not. This latter group is, for the most part, the product of the crazed imagination that comes to every golfer at roughly three o'clock in the morning!

Some formats you may be familiar with already, some you will never have read before, some you will quite possibly hope never to read again. Do, however, try some of these new games. Familiarity often really does breed at least some small contempt, and by trying out some, if not all, of these games then, if nothing else, you may well return to your more frequent forms of play with a renewed enthusiasm for the tried and trusted. Remember that nothing in any game is set in stone. Of course the rules must be applied strictly if you are playing in a competition, but outside this environment it can be fun to literally play around with the original concept of the grand old game. After all, this original concept only grew out of people messing about in the first place with a few holes, a stick of some sort, and a ball. The Old Course at St. Andrews may be the most historic and famous course on the planet but it is, despite much tweaking over the last couple of hundred years, still essentially a stretch of Scottish linksland that was originally sculpted into something like its present shape by a wind that can howl in off the sea and the scrapings of sheep anxious to locate some shelter.

One final word: throughout this book I use the masculine pronoun. This is not to ignore the millions of women who play golf, it is just that it becomes tiresome to write constantly "he or she," "him or her," etc. So if you are female please accept my explanation and please read the feminine form into my phraseology throughout. You could start by returning to the advice Snead gave Janzen earlier. Only in this instance replace "woman" with "man." Whatever your gender, enjoy your golf.

And remember that, as a rule, it is only a game …

THE RULES

HERE are 34 Rules of Golf. So why am I starting here with Rule 5 and ending with Rule 28? Because these are the rules that actually affect what you play with (the ball) and what you do, or don't do, with that ball when actually playing the game. The other ten rules cover the main ways—stroke play, match play, etc.—in which the game is played, the clubs used, the method by which a committee works, and various disputes and decisions. It's not that you do not need to know these, but they are not essential and, one way or another, most are explained elsewhere, and what I am trying to do here is to improve your knowledge of the rules that really will affect you, your playing partners, and your score. In other words these rules add up to the serious stuff.

RULE 5...THE BALL

FEW amateur golfers ever really consider the ball they use. They should. Depending on your ability, there are many different types of balls from which to choose. Some are harder than others, some have more dimples, or dimples of a different type, some are designed principally for distance, some offer greater "feel," and in turn this may help you play one of those delicate shots from around the green. Now this is all very well—and certainly offers up almost limitless opportunities for an especially informed dullard to bore opponents to death during a round—but the average player is happy to play with almost anything as long as it is, usually, white, round, and did not cost a second mortgage. The ball companies may spend fortunes on player endorsement and subsequent advertising, but to their great chagrin the ball type that consistently tops the "Average Player's Favorite Ball" poll is the one that he found while searching for the drive he sliced off the fourth tee yesterday. With balls now costing anything up to several dollars each these days, this is hardly surprising. Armed with this "free" ball our hero is also freed up to give it a whack, because losing this baby is not like having your pocket picked.

However, whether bought or found, white, yellow, or pink, the ball must conform to some rather strict rules. It must be not less than 1.68 inches in diameter, and it must not weigh more than 1.62 ounces. For the seriously technically minded this ball also must not be able to exceed 250 feet·per second as an initial velocity. Don't worry about this, however, as you are unlikely ever to be able to crank up your clubhead speed so that your ball comes anywhere close to this limit. Even attempting it may cause lingering internal injury.

On the other hand, you may have an enviable ability to thin an iron shot. This is not just (a) annoying and (b) embarrassing; it may also offer up option (c), which is to say you have cut a gash into the ball. If you think this has happened then the rule governing the ball is crystal clear:

you must alert your opponent that you feel a foul misdeed has occurred, mark your ball carefully, preferably in his presence, and then pick it up for inspection.

If everyone agrees that the ball is damaged and, crucially, "unfit for play" because it is cut, cracked, or otherwise then you may replace it. Be warned: you must have an interested witness to all these moves before you even touch the original ball or you will be docked a stroke or, in match play, lose that particular hole.

This is the bad news. The good news is that if you ever hit the ball and it breaks into pieces then the authorities, for once, have decided to cast a sympathetic eye on the event and you may replay your stroke with a replacement ball from the same spot.

One final point: you must always be able to identify your ball. Now you may feel that knowing the manufacturer's name and whatever number the ball carries (usually 1 through 4) is sufficient, but it is actually far from rare for two players in the same group to be playing identical balls. Especially if you get through half-a-dozen balls of assorted varieties in the course of a round.

Either mark your ball with a suitable pen yourself (as the pros do) or state its type and number before you play it so that if someone else has the same ball then he may replace it. If you cannot definitely identify your ball then it is deemed lost.

RULE 6...THE PLAYER

MORE than any other game, golf is an exercise in self-policing. YOU are the player and YOU must ensure that lurking somewhere is a knowledge of the rules and that you play within these parameters. There are no excuses. Unlike life, golf is a black-and-white affair. Like life, however, it frequently appears to be hugely unfair. This, of course, is part of its attraction. Enthusiastic golfers do not have to be sadomasochists but, in my experience, it helps.

As the player you should know your handicap and enter this on a scorecard. Failure to do so in a competition will mean disqualification. Entering the wrong scorecard brings the same penalty. You should also be punctual for your tee time, preferably a few minutes early. However, if you arrive within five minutes of this time and have a good excuse—"needed to drop wife off at hospital for birth of first child on the way," this sort of thing—then an official may (I stress *may*) allow you to play anyway after suffering a two-stroke penalty or, in match play, loss of the first hole. On the other hand they may decide that, as you've had nine months to prepare for the birth of this child, you are disqualified.

Make sure you know your score on each hole and record it. If you hand in a card that has a score against one hole that is lower than that actually taken then you are disqualified. If, however, a hole has a score higher than the one managed then the higher score stands. If each hole score is correct but you, or your opponent, have added them up incorrectly then no worries, because it is the competition committee's responsibility to ensure the numbers add up. It is always best to check an opponent's score with him before entering it onto the card and to make sure he concurs with your score.

Caddies are wonderful people. At least often they are. Sometimes, however, a caddie can be more hindrance than help. The fact is that as far as the Rules of Golf are concerned then a caddie is as much an extension of the player as that player's right hand. So if a caddie breaks a rule he does so on your behalf and YOU suffer the penalty.

PLAYERS' RESPONSIBILITIES
As a player you are expected to:
- *Know your handicap and enter it on your scorecard*
- *Be punctual for your tee time*
- *Know your score on each hole and record it correctly on your scorecard*
- *Play at a decent pace*

You are also responsible for a decent pace of play. This may be determined by a committee beforehand or by how much you are delaying the group behind. Just because Jack Nicklaus won 18 majors taking several hours over each putt does not mean you can. Always remember that you are not, and never will be, Jack Nicklaus and that you are playing in

FROM 13 TO 34

*THE HONOURABLE Company of Edinburgh Golfers—more
commonly known as Muirfield Golf Club—compiled The First
Rules of Golf, way back in 1774.*

*This was hardly surprising, as Muirfield has long been known
throughout the world as a sort of rest home or recreational center
for the Edinburgh legal profession, and lawyers, as we all know,
like nothing better than to sit around deconstructing simple
sentences in plain, understandable English and then reconstructing
them in such a way that we, the hoi polloi, have to pay them over
the odds to explain to us what it all means.*

*What may be surprising now, however, is that originally there
were just 13 Rules, and one of these was no more than a local
rule governing what to do if a ball entered one of the ditches
embroidering this wonderful links.*

*Since these original dozen Rules burst upon an unsuspecting
world the lawyers have never stopped beavering away so that we
now may enjoy a total of 34 Rules, even more definitions, and god
knows how many clauses, subclauses, and appendices. On top of
this we may embrace a platoon of unwieldy volumes of case law in
the form of Decisions that have been arrived at over many years by
the Rules of Golf Committee on appeal.*

the monthly club tournament and not The Open Championship. Playing slowly is a disease and should be avoided. It can bring penalties or even disqualification so get a move on. On the other hand it can be annoying to have a group behind who seem more intent on trotting between shots than playing the game. No real penalty here but it does come under etiquette and the penalty may be social exile.

As a player you will sometimes be playing poorly when heavy rain strikes. This is truly miserable. However, unless the committee decides that flooding has made the course unplayable, you must play on.

Suffering is part of golf. Wet weather is no reason to call a halt, unless it is a friendly game in which case you would be crazy to carry on. If lightning is feared, however, then everyone is entitled to drop their clubs and run for cover. Not entitled, required. And don't then stand under a tree or carry 14 metal clubs. The penalty for these transgressions may be particularly severe.

RULE 7...PRACTICE

THE AVERAGE golfer does not really practice. He plays. Sometimes, however, he will practice while he plays. This is a minefield. The smartest move is to assume that basically, in stroke play competition, you may not practice at all during play. The rule states you may not practice on the course on any day of the competition.

PRACTICE PENALTY
Practice means taking a stroke at a ball other than if it is the ball in play and the stroke is integral to your play. Even if you find an old ball lying somewhere, resist the temptation to hit it as this may be construed as practice. Just ignore it. Any transgression of this rule can result in disqualification.

Remember: A casual flick of a practice ball back to the range may be OK, but hit it back with a full swing and you have broken the rule.

Minus a ball, you may take as many practice swings as you like as long as they are not holding up play, endangering your playing partners, or digging up the turf. You may swing at daisies, dandelions, chestnuts, leaves, rabbit droppings, or other natural, or unnatural, paraphernalia lying around. You may practice swing in a hazard but you must not touch the sand, the ground, or the water. The penalty is two strokes. You may, however, practice putt or chip on or near a green or near the next tee once that hole has been completed but only if it is not holding up play for anyone. The committee retains the right to decide and so I recommend never practicing in this manner.

In match play the natural universe described above is turned upside down in one particular regard. Here you may practice on the course prior to competing on the actual day of competition. Apart from this the rule, as described, works the same way except that if you take a minute to have a practice whack out of a bunker, or other hazard, then you forfeit a hole. Not the one you've just played, assuming you have won it, but the next hole. Just to add further modest confusion to the chaos already achieved in explaining this rule, it is worth pointing out that the "no practice on the course in stroke play" bit is clouded by the fact that you may, while waiting to begin such a round, practice chip or putt by or near the first tee. Personally, I wouldn't bother. Better to practice on a practice range or putting green where you may do what you want and not risk any penalty.

RULE 8...ADVICE

OFFERING, or seeking, advice while on the course is a wonderful area of confusion for anyone who has ever stepped on a golf course. If you are playing someone in a match and, after several holes of ill-disguised snickering at what passes laughably as your swing, this opponent suddenly has an attack of sympathy and points out that your left hand is so far under the shaft he wonders how you have not broken a bone, or perhaps that your head is coming up faster than a rising desert sun, then you may claim that hole.

In stroke play you may penalize this guy two shots. However, in the interests of maintaining the game's fair image do remember to thank him as well. Especially if the advice works.

The point here is that you have not asked for advice and he is not permitted to give it. On the other hand, if you ask him to help out then he may penalize you. This rule has not been known to forge strong friendships.

If you are a member of a team and there is a nonplaying captain then you may ask him as well although you will probably find he is in the bar. But woe to everyone if a playing partner or friendly caddie points out the line of a putt and actually touches the intended line. Two strokes or loss of hole for this one, I'm afraid.

Meanwhile, you may ask anyone, on your side or not, what the line is or how far it is to the target from, say, a tree or bush or a sprinkler head. This, wise men have decided after much deliberation and quite a lot of port, is "public information." Do not, however, ask how far it is to the hole or green from where your BALL lies or you will be in trouble again. Oh, and if someone helpfully stands on a hill to signpost the correct flightpath to the flag, then make sure he has moved away before you swing otherwise you will be up before the judge again.

One final warning: do not ask an opponent what club he has just used. You may, however, walk over and peer into his bag to ascertain this fact for yourself. To counter this intrusion he may cover his clubs with a towel or, *in extremis*, turn the bag upside down and hide it under a thorn bush. You may now not remove this towel or touch his equipment in any way. You may well also decide never to play with this guy again. Almost certainly he will already have decided never to play with you again.

RULE 9...INFORMATION

THIS is perhaps the most obvious rule of all the Rules of Golf inasmuch as all it really requires is that you are numerate and one hundred percent honest. There is, however, a significant difference in the way in which it is applied to either stroke play or match play.

In match play a player must always give an accurate reply when an opponent asks how many strokes have been played. If you make an honest mistake but correct it before your opponent plays his shot then there is no penalty. If he has played already then you lose that hole because his strategy may have been seriously affected by how he judges the situation and what sort of shot he plays next.

In the former your marker should have a knowledge of how many strokes you are taking but he is naturally entitled to confirm this with you. A dishonest reply—that is, claiming fewer strokes than you actually took after emerging from a patch of dense woodland, for example—is simply cheating and should bring all expected penalties from disqualification to social exclusion. One of the basic principles of golf is honesty. Frankly, there are too many opportunities to cheat during a four-hour round over several miles of real estate for the game's rulers not to stamp very hard indeed on any willful offenders.

I say willful because sometimes, perhaps even often, many of us unwittingly underscore a hole simply because we have transgressed some rule but through ignorance have not realized. While this may bring sympathy rather than tarring and feathering if it does come to light, the penalty will still be imposed retrospectively if at all practical and possible.

So if asked by a marker what you have scored you must include any penalty shots incurred when you make your reply. This is common sense really, certainly moral sense, but worth bearing in mind.

RULE 10...ORDER OF PLAY

PLAYING first off the first tee means you have the "honor." Who gets it to begin with? Well, if there is a start sheet then it is the first name down who takes the honor. Similarly in match play it is the first name on the draw sheet who hits the opening shot. If neither is available then you can either just get on with it as the mood takes your group or you may draw lots, toss a coin, or ask a series of penetrating questions on the geophysical makeup of the Galapagos Islands. Guessing the color of each other's socks has been known to work well too.

ON THE TEE
The player who has the "honor" plays first. The honor is retained until another player betters his score on a hole, or in match play until the "honor" player loses a hole.

THROUGH THE GREEN
The ball lying farthest away from the hole should be played first.

Once you have the "honor" you retain it as long as no one betters your score on a hole, or in match play until you lose a hole. If someone plays out of order then there is no penalty except that this person has just exhibited extreme rudeness. However, a committee may later decide this happened in order to advantage an individual or the group in some way—wind direction, club needed to reach green, and so on—and the group may well be disqualified, so always play in order. In match play your opponent has the right to demand you replay a shot played out of turn, and may do so unless you have just sliced it out of bounds, in which case he is permitted to remind you of both your lack of etiquette and your lack of talent. In most cases this should be worth the next two holes to him—at least.

Away from the tee it is the ball farthest from the hole that should be played first. In match play this is absolutely required. If two balls appear to be equidistant from the target then get the Galapagos Island quiz book out again. If, however, the balls are equidistant but one would interfere with either the swing or stance of a player, then the other ball should be played.

Farthest from the hole works on the putting green as well, with the proviso that in stroke play you have the right to putt out once you start, but in match play you must play strictly in order. Even if the ball is only a few inches away from the hole, you must mark it unless the next putt has

A CHAMP'S DECISION IS FINAL

SOMETIMES the Rules do not matter a tuppenny damn. Especially on the Portuguese Algarve. Specifically at the glorious Penina Championship course that was designed by triple British Open Champion Henry Cotton, who transformed a bunch of paddy fields into a formidable test of golf.

It was here over the last decade of his life that I had an annual match with Henry. At stake each time was a 10,000-escudo note, and my ambition was to beat the aging maestro and then have him autograph the note. I never managed to do it although I came very close once. This moment came when, 17 holes played and the match halved, I lay 15 feet from the final hole in three while Henry was some 50 feet adrift in the same number of shots. When his first putt came up short by some six feet, leaving him an exquisitely curling putt for his par, I knew that I was in with a serious chance of success. If Henry missed, which seemed likely, and I got down in at least two, also likely, I'd be able to choose the frame for my signed banknote.

As he approached this putt Henry looked at me. For my part I looked away. All I heard was a grunt as he bent down and then, to my astonishment, he picked up his ball, explaining, "I hope you don't mind old boy but I always feel I've holed enough of these in my career never again to have to prove I can do it." Naturally, I missed my birdie putt and the match was halved. Triple Open champs sometimes operate under their own rules and who are we to argue?

been conceded, which it should be unless your opponent is related to the guy who tried to hide his clubs under a thorn bush during the explanation of Rule 8. If you hole even the shortest putt without "permission" then an unscrupulous opponent may claim the hole.

If you need to play either a provisional drive or straightforward second tee shot then you must wait until everyone else has played their drives. If a provisional, you must make everyone aware of this in a clear voice. Failure to do so clearly and audibly may lead to all sorts of shenanigans if the first ball is found in an eminently playable position, and you may have to play your second ball, which inevitably has found its way into a buried lie in a deep bunker.

RULE 11...THE TEEING GROUND

PRETTY OBVIOUS this one. At least inasmuch as any of these rules are pretty obvious. The teeing ground is that area set aside for, guess what, teeing off. This is accomplished by a greenkeeper (not, note, a teekeeper) placing a couple of markers in the ground.

This, for those of you unfamiliar with the concept, can be vividly advantageous depending on the natural shape of your usual shot and the layout of the hole you are playing. For example, if you, as most of us do, hit a natural fade thanks to an out-to-in swing, a fade that sometimes turns into a real slice, then basically, you are better advised to tee up your ball to the right of any teeing ground and aim out towards the left of the fairway because this allows a greater depth of fairway for the ball to hit. The opposite is clearly true if you hit a draw, while if you hit the ball dead straight the rest of us would like to know how the hell you manage this.

> You must not play forward of the line drawn between the tee markers, and you must not go more than two club lengths back from them. You may, however, stand outside this area to hit your drive as long as the ball itself is inside this invisible rectangle.

If in match play you play the ball from either too far forward or too far behind the tee markers then your opponent has the right to require you to replay the shot. This he will do unless, of course, you've just whacked the damn thing into trouble. There is, however, no formal penalty, although the feeling of stupidity that envelops you as you tee up a second ball at his request is likely to cause you all sorts of mental problems. In stroke play it is formally laid down that, no matter what the reason for anyone teeing off outside the prescribed area, he must be docked two strokes and have to play another ball from within the tee box.

One final thought: Greenkeepers sometimes place tee markers while still under the influence of the previous evening's revelry, and so they appear to the player's eye to be out of line. Tough. Complain later to the head greenkeeper or secretary, or write a letter to your local paper, but do not attempt to remedy this situation by moving the markers or you may be penalized. Oh, and if you accidentally knock your ball off its tee and someone says "one" then please feel free to fall over in a fit of laughter for at least five minutes.

RULE 12...SEARCHING FOR AND IDENTIFYING YOUR BALL

SOMETIMES balls come to rest in heavy rough, in water or in a hazard in such a way as you cannot definitely identify it as your ball. This is both infuriating and dangerous territory and challenges all but the most keenly sighted. In a bunker you may probe for the ball. If found you can hit it and if it turns out not to be your ball there is no penalty. In a hazard you may not probe but again if you find a ball, hit it and then discover it is not yours, there is no penalty and you can return to the search.

PICKING UP THE BALL
Unless you are in a hazard, you may pick up your ball in order to identify it but it must be marked and replaced in exactly the same spot.

If the ball is in water then you may probe for it with your club but if you intend having a go at it despite getting wet in the process then, if moved, it must be rolled back to where it was originally found. It is inadvisable to try to hit a ball out of water unless the situation is desperate, the sun is shining and you are a very, very poor loser.

If your ball has buried itself in a bunker you may scrape away such sand as is needed to see that there is a ball present, then re-cover it and play it. If it turns out not to be your ball there is no penalty. Go back and find yours and play on. For this reason it is always sensible to identify that it really was your ball before hitting it again from outside the hazard.

In heavy rough you may move, say, long grass or a branch, but only to the extent that is necessary to find and identify your ball. Don't break any growing thing or bend it so it is no longer affecting the ball or its exit route. You may pick up the ball to make sure it is yours but first tell someone else what you are doing so they can act as a witness and mark it so that it can be replaced exactly. You can't clean it. Golf can be a dirty game sometimes.

RULE 13...BALL PLAYED AS IT LIES

THIS, you will not be surprised, can sound complicated. In fact it is simple. The original and best way to play golf is to hit the ball off the tee, find it, and hit it again. This means precisely that and if you play like this then you do not need to know any rules at all. However, you cannot improve in any way the manner in which the ball is lying, the ground upon which you stand, the line of your intended swing, or the target line the ball will hopefully follow.

Do not even think of getting out that Swiss Army Knife and lopping off a few branches or stamping around your ball with a heavy foot so the grass is trampled down and your clubhead can more cleanly strike the ball. This is not merely environmentally unfriendly, this is cheating.

If you have to pick and drop then do not first improve the area upon which the ball is going to be dropped. It is sensible though to have a good look at the legal drop area to see what is the absolute best place on which to TRY to drop the ball. This is not cheating, this is astute.

If you have to, back into bushes or trees carefully, causing as little disturbance as possible as you take your stance, during which process you cannot deliberately step on a branch or whatever so that it is removed from harm's way. It's all common sense really.

In a hazard you are not allowed to touch the ground with your club so if you take a practice swing make sure the clubhead stays well clear. In fact it is much better not to practice at all in a hazard. If there is a stone in front of your ball then tough; this is a natural object or, in golfrulespeak, a "loose impediment". Cigar butts, discarded bottles, cans, and the like are "movable obstructions" and may be picked up—but if Mother Nature put something in the hazard then there it must remain.

RULE 14...STRIKING THE BALL

ESSENTIALLY the action of striking the ball has to be a deliberate downward movement with the intention of hitting it, and this is why if you accidentally nudge it off a tee peg there is no penalty involved. What you are not allowed to do is to push or scoop the ball, so you may not place the clubface directly behind the ball and scoop it into the air. Ah, but what if the ball is up against, say, a wall in such a way that as you can get the clubface behind it to push or scoop it forward? Isn't it fair in this circumstance to do so? The answer is NO. If you cannot make a stroke—and this may involve swinging the clubface into the ball from a few inches away—then you will have to declare it unplayable and drop away under penalty. Otherwise you will be penalized a shot and the ball will be replaced where it was.

While hitting your shot you may not have any added protection from the elements. So while a caddie may hold an umbrella over you right up to the instant you begin your swing he must then walk away while the stroke is played.

You cannot even use a towel to kneel on to avoid getting your knees wet or trousers soiled, as Craig Stadler discovered when he did so during when he did so during the 1987 Buick Invitational at Torrey Pines and some sharp-eyed television viewer rang in to complain. Stadler was subsequently disqualified for returning an incorrect score and lost many thousands of dollars in prize money.

Occasionally when playing a delicate pitch or bunker shot you will decelerate the club so much that you hit the ball more than once. This, no matter how many times you actually strike the ball, incurs a single penalty shot and you then play the ball from where it has landed. The only circumstance under which you may hit a moving ball is if it is in water, but you must not wait until the ball has moved into an advantageous position. By the way, if your ball falls off its tee during your swing and you fail to stop in time before striking it then it still counts as a stroke. If, however, you manage to abort your swing before you reach the ball – or the tee in this instance – then you have not made a stroke and may start again.

RULE 15...PLAYING THE WRONG BALL

OKAY, let's define the correct ball first ... this is the ball that is hit off the tee, or a replacement ball if the tee ball is lost, is knocked irretrievably out of bounds, or is, by agreement, so damaged for whatever reason that it needs to be changed.

ACCIDENTAL PLAY OF OPPONENT'S BALL
- *Match play — lose the hole*
- *Stroke play — two-stroke penalty*

Be careful here because in match play if you carelessly "exchange" balls then it is the first one to make a stroke at the wrong ball who is penalized. If this cannot be determined—and it's hard to see why not—then you both must play out the hole with the balls you have now adopted. When the wrong ball is played then the player whose ball it is must play a ball from the correct spot where this infringement took place.

Incidentally, if you are playing a four-ball better-ball match then the partner of the person penalized does not suffer apart from the obvious disadvantage of having to play the other two guys on his own.

And remember, you cannot be penalized for playing a wrong ball out of a hazard, but you must not continue to play it. If this turns out to be another group member's ball then he must replace it as close as possible to the original spot and play on without penalty.

Very occasionally you may find yourself in a stroke-play competition and be unsure of a rule following some incident or other. In this instance you may play out the hole with two balls but as long as you inform the other player what is going on before doing anything then you should be okay.

RULE 16...THE PUTTING GREEN

BY NOW, if you have plowed through all the previous pages, it will have dawned on you that you are unlikely to ever actually make it to the green. Worry not, you will always do this. Eventually. Once there, the rules governing play are simple enough.

If you wish you may mark, lift, and clean your ball. You may also repair an old hole plug or a pitch mark (actually, always try to repair two pitch marks, yours and one that some other ignoramus has neglected to fix—if you do this then the greenkeeper will thrice bless you). And you may mark the ball behind, to the side, or in front, although what is the point in not always marking it behind? Answer: none.

> ## ON THE GREEN YOU MAY:
> - mark the ball behind, to the side, or in front
> - mark, lift, and clean your ball
> - repair an old hole plug or a pitch mark

Do not touch the line of your, or anyone else's, putt unless you are removing a movable obstruction or a loose impediment such as a leaf or a twig or you are repairing a pitch mark. Don't ever try to test the surface of the green in any way, don't stand astride, or on, the line, don't touch the green when indicating the line for a partner, don't brush aside any early morning dew or frost, and don't wait forever, or jump up and down, to see if a ball that is hanging over the hole drops. In this instance you have the time it takes to walk to the hole and then 10 seconds; if the ball drops after this then you have to add another stroke to your score.

Oh, and the other occasion on which you may touch the line is when measuring two putts to ascertain who goes first.

RULE 17...THE FLAGSTICK

THE FLAGSTICK may seem an innocent enough object, no more than a guide to where the hole is on the green. Wrong. The flagstick is an integral part of the game and carries its own set of rules. It may often be your friend, as when an approach shot that would have carried through the green strikes the pole and comes to rest a few inches away, but it may also be your enemy.

OFF THE GREEN
When off the green you have three options:
- *leave the flagstick where it is*
- *have it attended*
- *have it taken out*

If attended, however, then both the flagstick and the attendee must not be struck by your ball. It does not matter if the person appointed by you to attend the stick slips into an unexpected catatonic trance and so fails to (a) remove

FLAG FIASCO

IT IS NOT, at least as I understand it, a Rule, but it is common sense to have only 18 visible flags on any one course. However, this is not always the case.

Take the strange matter of Ronan Rafferty and the mystery fluttering. The Irishman was a young emerging golfer in the early 1980s after an amateur career that had been the right side of terrific. When he turned professional this amateur record meant that Rafferty was under a much bigger spotlight than is usual, for most rookie pros have at least some time to learn their craft without the media peering too closely into what is happening.

Not so Rafferty and especially not when he played in the Bob Hope Classic at the RAC Club in southern England. He was on fire that day, making birdie after birdie so that by the time he reached the closing holes he was in the lead. Then, apparently out of a clear blue sky, he dropped three strokes on one hole. What made this even more significant was that the hole in question was not a particularly challenging one, and when the score went up in the Media Tent every reporter sat up and took baleful-eyed notice. Asked how this had occurred he explained: "Well, my second shot was quite possibly the finest 3-wood I have ever hit in my life. It was hit absolutely solid and headed straight for the flag I'd spotted in the distance. Sadly, this flag was the one fluttering on top of a McDonald's hamburger tent and I never saw my ball again. I didn't even get a hamburger."

the flagstick as your ball trundles into the hole or (b) fails to move his body out of the path of your ball; and it strikes either animate or inanimate object and in match play you lose the hole, in stroke play you incur a two-shot penalty.

ON THE GREEN
Once on the green your options are reduced to:
- *have it attended*
- *have it taken out*

Be careful, even if it is lying innocently on the ground and you strike the flag or pole then the same penalties are incurred. The one exception to this is an approach shot to an elevated green where all or part of the flagstick is not visible. In this case you may have someone stand over the hole and raise the flagstick aloft. Here they may remain, and if your ball hits either object then no penalty is suffered although there may be a hospital bill to pay.

Incidentally, not all sticks have flags on top of them. Several golf clubs, most notably Merion Golf Club, near Philadelphia, have baskets on top of the pole. This is believed to have stemmed from the original Scottish golf courses where lobster pots were often placed on top of sticks to make the hole stand out more clearly. Purists argue that a basket is an infinitely better option than a flag as the former may be seen from any angle and does not help a player to judge either wind direction or strength. In the unlikely, but not entirely inconceivable, event of a ball getting lodged in a basket the rules permit the ball to be placed on the edge of the hole without penalty. Sometimes, it is very nearly a fair game.

RULE 18...BALL AT REST MOVED

THE BALL is deemed to have moved when it does just that ... by this I mean it actually has to MOVE, not oscillate, vibrate, or shimmy a bit. If it does move and you, your equipment, your shortsighted partner, or your careless caddie have caused it to move then you suffer a stroke penalty. If someone, or something, else causes it to move then no one suffers anything and you just replace it.

PENALTY FOR BALL AT REST MOVED
If your equipment, your partner, or your caddie cause the ball to move, you suffer a one-stroke penalty

All sorts of things move balls. Sometimes it can be a greenkeeper, occasionally a dog or a cat, even the odd crow has been known to swoop and make off with a ball, which is about as much fun as it ever gets for a crow. Once in South Africa I had my ball nicked by a cheeky monkey and while in Florida I have been happy to donate the ball to a sunbathing alligator, which I felt was too close for comfort and for which there was no penalty as I could claim my life was under threat. Well, that's my story and I'm sticking to it.

It's the usual tale in a hazard or on the green where there is no penalty, although if it is accidentally moved on the green while carrying out a legitimate move (like marking it or measuring) the ball must be replaced before being played.

If your ball moves after you've addressed it then you are held responsible and it must be replaced under a one-shot penalty. If it moves mid-swing and you cannot help but hit it then you play it from where it comes to rest but only after adding a penalty shot. This is a serious test of character so make sure you don't fail it.

Arnold Palmer once played what appeared to be a perfect shot out of a cavernous pot bunker during an Open Championship. However, having clambered up from the bottom of the abyss, he reported that the ball had moved and to add a penalty shot. Palmer continues to earn millions because of his character and honesty AND he sleeps at night.

One final thought: If you accidentally kick your ball while searching for it then you are penalized a shot. However, if you stand on it what do you do? Strictly speaking the ball must have moved, if only downward, but (a) this is now likely to be an even more difficult lie and (b) it might have sprung back into its original position. Who knows? Examine your conscience at the time and make a decision. Most of us would agree no penalty is required. However I should add that the European Tour's chief referee John Paramor would take the opposite view and conclude that, as you could not prove otherwise, you should presume it has moved and add a penalty. I love playing with John.

RULE 19... BALL IN MOTION DEFLECTED OR STOPPED

YOU'VE just hit the approach shot of your life and as the ball zeroes in on the green a bird in flight swoops by. Ball hits bird and drops short. Tough. And before you scream at the injustice, consider this: If the same bird had deflected your ball into the hole then this, too, would count. This is called "the rub of the green," a phrase first encountered in some written regulations at St. Andrews in 1812 that states: "Whatever happens to a ball by accident must be considered a rub of the green."

This may be an abiding, tough-love outlook on life but it also captures the fact that while golf is a finely regulated game it never was meant to be a fair one. Or unfair for that matter. At the philosophical heart of the game is the thought that stuff happens so, for the most part, just grit your teeth and get on with it.

If an animal, bird, or passing idiot picks up your ball and makes off with it and you see the incident, then drop another ball where this occurred. If it happens on the green then place rather than drop the ball. If you strike the ball and it hits your equipment, your partner, or caddie then you lose the hole in match play or suffer a two-shot penalty in stroke play and then you have to play the ball from where it lies. If it accidentally thumps into an opponent then you may either play it as it lies or cancel that stroke and replay it before anyone else plays. First, though, apologize.

Occasionally your ball will hit another ball that is at rest. No penalty here although the first ball may be replaced on its original spot. On the green, however you will lose the hole or suffer a two-shot penalty, so if you think there is the slightest risk of your putt hitting another ball then ask for it to be marked. Otherwise you will be penalized.

RULE 20...LIFTING AND DROPPING AND OTHER STUFF

THE OFFICIAL rule book meanders on forever on the vexed question of lifting your ball and dropping it again. No wonder, for this is a minefield full of unexploded bombs filled with doubt and danger. Don't worry, it will be okay.

If, for some reason, you need to lift and drop then the first thing to do is to mark the spot from which you are lifting your ball. This is not a requirement, but a suggestion, and the reason for this is that it rules out an awful lot of subsequent argument.

> ## TO DROP THE BALL YOU MUST:
> - *stand erect*
> - *hold your arm out at shoulder length*
> - *let go of the ball*
>
> Get this wrong and you are penalized a stroke if you hit it.

If the ball hits you or yours on its way to the ground, or indeed bounces up and strikes, then you have to drop it again. No penalty. And no limit to the number of times you may carry out this procedure.

Once dropped, the ball must not have ended up nearer the hole, not even by a millimetre. This is why you marked it in the first place. Everyone can see, no one can moan. You must re-drop if the ball rolls into a hazard or out of a hazard; if it rolls on to the green (if you'd been on the green in the first place you would have placed it, not dropped – remember?); if it rolls out of bounds (even the sadists who govern golf find this unacceptably unfair); if it ends up more than two club lengths from where it first strikes the ground or, of course, if it ends up nearer the hole. However, if you have taken relief from an unplayable lie and then drop it into an unplayable lie again relief will cost you another penalty shot.

GET INTO THE GROOVE

MAKING certain you play with legal clubs and balls is so blindingly obvious that it is rarely mentioned in polite society, even if nowadays there is increasing scrutiny of the thin-faced drivers that manufacturers are turning out, which sometimes circumvent the close parameters established for these faces and help give a modern ball more "hang time" in the air so that the most prodigious hitters can keep a ball up there for 300 yards and more. The PGA Tour has introduced random testing of drivers following complaints from some players that others were illegally gaining an advantage and even Tiger Woods' driver has been tested. And, it must be added, found to be legal.

However, even the most scrupulous of golfers can innocently make a mistake. Take Tom Watson for example. Long before thin-faced, or even two-faced drivers hit the scene, the five-time British Open champ won the 1977 Masters and then The British Open and was playing in the PGA Championship that year when it was discovered that the clubs he had used for both victories were illegal as they had grooves that exceeded the permitted specifications of the time.

An upset Watson then had the set he had used two years earlier to win his first British Open flown out for inspection and these too were found to be illegal. Fortunately the authorities decided there should be no retrospective action and Watson kept his titles, even if his innocent transgression hung around his neck for some time and encouraged some totally unnecessary bickering from others in the lockerroom.

In each of these scenarios you may have no more than two attempts at an acceptable drop, after which you must place the ball on the nearest spot affording relief from your marker. If, in this process, you lose your ball then you can use another ball without penalty.

The rules allow for your partner to place or replace your ball. Ignore this. Always do it yourself. And if you accidentally move a marker when lifting the ball then you must replace the marker in its original spot or it's a penalty shot. If you have to mark your ball in a bunker because, say, it would interfere with another's shot then you are entitled to replace it in such a way as to recreate the original lie. This may mean raking the sand if it has been ruffled by the other shot or by half-burying it again if that is how you found it.

If the ball will not stay on its spot when you replace it—on a severely sloping green or hillside for example—then you may place it as close as possible to where it will stay put. It helps to confer with an opponent when doing this. And if you have to retreat to replay a shot—maybe you've discovered you are out of bounds—then you must drop the ball as near as possible to the original spot. Again, check with your opponent that he agrees with the selected area. Oh, and if you were in a bunker then you still must drop the ball from shoulder height even if this means you end up plugged. If you deliberately drop in an advantageous but wrong area and play the ball then you will be disqualified.

RULE 21...CLEANING THE BALL

ONCE the ball is on the green you may lift and clean it to your heart's content. Elsewhere it is not quite so simple.

You must not clean the ball if you have picked it up to check some suspected damage. However, if picked up in the process of identification then you may clean the ball BUT only to the extent needed to confirm it is yours, so don't wipe it all over with your towel or you're in trouble.

If you have to mark and lift the ball because it is interfering with play then hold it between thumb and forefinger before replacing it because it must go back on its spot in exactly the same condition it was in when it originally came to rest, and if there is a blob of mud stuck to the side then that must remain.

Often when there has been a lot of rain and the course is especially muddy, club officials will invoke the "lift and place" rule on the fairway. You are not required to lift and place—mark first and replace within six inches NOT nearer the hole—but if you do then you may clean mud or any other stuff off the ball before replacing it.

RULE 22...BALL ASSISTING OR INTERFERING WITH PLAY

THERE ARE still golfers alive who played the game under the old "stymie" rule whereby if an opponent's ball was in the way of your intended putt on the green then you could not demand that it be lifted and the marker moved to the side of your intended line. So you were "stymied" or "blocked." What fun that must have been at times until the rule was changed in the early 1950s.

During a recent Ryder Cup, Seve Ballesteros almost caused an international incident when he asked his singles opponent, Tom Lehman, to mark a six-inch putt rather than conceding such a tiddler as would be the norm. Seve's thinking was that Lehman's marker would help him with the line of the putt he now had to hit. Lehman did not get this and felt that the Spaniard was insulting his ability to hole out from six inches, and there ensued a serious, heated exchange. Seve, of course, was within his match play rights but was he being "fair"? Or was he just trying to wind up an opponent as often happens in these matches. As ever the line betwixt fairness and gamesmanship remains blurred.

Now if you feel that your opponent's ball is lying in such a way that it disadvantages you then you can ask him to mark it and lift it. He cannot, of course, clean it—except if the ball lies on the green. I mention the green because here, though there may be no physical interference, you may feel that you can see another ball out of the corner of your eye and that it is a distraction. Don't hesitate to have it marked and lifted. Apart from anything else it will impress on your opponent that you are a serious player. Or an annoying jerk.

If, on the other hand, you suspect that your ball is in some way assisting your opponent then you may insist on marking and lifting. Indeed, in a stroke-play event you may play your ball first if you wish although in match play you do not have this option. As ever, a refined sense of fairness permeates everything here.

RULE 23...LOOSE IMPEDIMENTS

LOOSE impediments do exactly what it says on the label. They are natural objects—that is to say, the product of nature rather than man—and include all the usual stuff from leaves to twigs to huge branches and those rotten banana peels that seem to litter so many courses ever since the world's top professionals started eating them halfway through their rounds. As long as the loose impediment isn't fixed or growing, isn't solidly embedded in the ground or stuck solidly to your ball (you may encourage a live insect to get off the ball but not remove a dead, squashed one that is adhering to the surface) then you may remove said object without penalty.

However—and by now you must have known this was coming—if by removing the loose impediment you cause your ball to move then you suffer a stroke penalty and then you must replace it on the exact spot it has just left or you will be punished again. So always take care when moving something and if you have a tiny doubt about whether or not the ball may be affected then leave well alone. It's not worth the possible anguish.

And be aware that, while sand or soil is considered a loose impediment on the green and may be brushed aside, it may not be touched anywhere else. How many times have you seen someone brush away a line of bunker sand from the path of the ball as a putt from just off the green is contemplated. If any of this sand is on the fringe—even by half an inch—then the sweeper has transgressed.

If you are nutty enough to play a lot of winter golf then it is likely you will encounter early morning frost. Don't touch the stuff. This is not a loose impediment. Snow on the other hand may be brushed away or you may even treat it as casual water and seek the nearest point of relief. Personally, I'd recommend staying in bed or, if you must have your quasi-golf fix, the clubhouse bar.

Remember you may not touch any loose impediment in a hazard. If this means you enter a bunker to discover a hefty branch has fallen in and your ball is nestling against it, then you either have to play it as it lies or take a penalty drop inside the hazard. Unless there is a local rule governing the removal of stones you should leave these alone too although most of us value both our eyesight and the condition of our wedges more than we worry about breaking this rule.

SPACED OUT

THE FIRST golf shot to be played outside of Planet Earth was executed by Captain Alan B. Shepard on the dusty surface of the moon in February 1971. In total the commander of the Apollo 14 spacecraft hit two balls and, using a one-handed swing (spacesuits, apparently, are even more cumbersome than raingear), he claims to have whacked the first ball some 200 yards with a makeshift club, a 6-iron head attached to a soil sampler—NASA bosses were not keen on their hero taking an actual normal shafted club with him so Shepard had to improvise his out-of-this-world device when he arrived at his historic destination.

Though that first shot was a beauty, the second effort he rather reassuringly shanked, much to the amusement of every golfer watching back on Earth. However, to celebrate this inaugural extraterrestrial game of golf, the Royal & Ancient Club sent the following telegram: "Warmest congratulations to all of you on your great achievement and safe return. Please refer to Rules of Golf *section on etiquette, para six, quote—before leaving a bunker a player should carefully fill in all holes made by him therein—unquote."*

Even at a distance of some 250,000 miles the Powers That Be still have their beady eyes on us it seems. On the other hand this message does go some way toward disproving the feeling in some quarters that the Blazers up in St. Andrews stumble through life minus a real sense of humor.

Unless you are playing in a competition have a word with your playing partner about the sensible thing to do.

RULE 24...OBSTRUCTIONS

THESE fall into two distinct types – the sort you may remove and the type you may remove your ball from. As distinct from the previous rule all these objects are artificial or man-made. The first species is made up of the flotsam and jetsam of modern life really, cans, bottles, cigarette packets or butts and so on. These, and their ilk, are all deemed movable for the simple reason they clearly are just that.

So move them and if your ball moves as well just replace it on its spot without penalty. If you think there is a good chance the ball might move then mark it first to avoid any possible argument. If your ball ends up either on, or even in, a movable obstruction then mark the spot as closely as possible and lift your ball while you sort it out. In this instance you then drop it where you honestly believe it would have been had the obstruction not been there, or the nearest point of relief.

Odd things are always happening on golf courses. For example, while playing with my sons at Wentworth in 2004, one of them struck a shot that travelled 150 yards and ended up in the basket of my cart. Of course I lied through my teeth and told him he had to play it as it lay. And, yes, I did consider driving into the nearest rough first.

If you find any movable obstructions in a hazard then you may remove these also but if the ball moves it must be replaced.

OBSTRUCTIONS
- *Moveable e.g. litter — remove the obstruction and replace your ball on its spot.*
- *Immovable e.g. sprinkler heads, markers — drop the ball within one club length of the nearest point of relief.*

Immovable obstructions. These sweeties lie all over a golf course. The most common are sprinkler heads, stone, or similar, distance markers, and those gravestone-type objects offering information about the hole to be played. If these, or their like, actually interfere with your swing, stance or, by proximity, your ball, then you may take relief by selecting the nearest point of relief, placing a tee peg on that spot, and then dropping within one club length.

Be aware though that it is not good enough to exaggerate your stance or swing to bring any of these obstructions into play, neither is it kosher to claim that if you thinned your shot you might hit the object. And if you find yourself up against a stake or post marking the out-of-bounds, then you may not move it. If you really cannot hit the ball then you have to take relief under a one-shot penalty.

RULE 25...ABNORMAL GROUND CONDITIONS, EMBEDDED BALL AND WRONG PUTTING GREEN

THIS RULE goes on forever so let me try to put it simply. The most common abnormal ground condition is when there is flooding, or casual water, after a hell of a lot of rain. In this instance you are allowed to take relief without penalty if you are on the fairway and water is either visible or becomes visible after you take your stance (that is, your weight has brought it to the surface). Once again your point of relief will be the dry area closest to where your ball rested but not nearer the hole. If you wish to be formal, or it's a proper competition, you must mark this with a tee peg, measure off a club length, mark again, and then drop the ball between the two markers. It doesn't matter if it rolls up to another club length away as long as it hit the ground between these two fixed points.

On the green you do not have to be actually in a puddle to lift and place elsewhere, for if there is water between you and the hole then you can move. But you must not place the ball anywhere nearer this hole and if that means moving back off the green then this is what you must do.

Perhaps the toughest rule in golf comes in this section. If a bunker is flooded to the extent that there is nowhere to take relief and you have to drop outside the hazard then it is a one-shot penalty. Always keep the line between your original position and the flag in mind when you drop. In other words you cannot now drop to the side of the bunker—the ball must remain between you and the target. How brilliantly unfair is this? But there you are. It will make you a better person eventually. Maybe.

It's better news where ground under repair is concerned. These areas are often marked either GUR and/or have a white line painted around them. Sometimes, however, the greenkeeper has merely piled some turf or dumped a load of grass cuttings. These too are usually GUR, and you may take unpenalized relief at the nearest spot but only if the stuff has been piled for removal and not merely abandoned.

If the ground is particularly soggy then your ball may plug. If it is in a mown area—and this is not only fairways but all actual closely MOWN areas including paths through rough—then you may lift, clean, and drop in the usual manner. If it is in the rough then the rules don't allow you to lift unless you are willing to pay the penalty of one shot. It's worth checking whether there is a local rule covering this.

If you end up on the wrong green then, to avoid damage to the surface, you must drop off the green not nearer the hole etc. If your ball, your stance, or your swing is affected by a burrow or a hole made by by a reptile or a bird (honest!), you can take relief with the eternal caveat that if you are in a bunker you must stay within it.

If you lose your ball in particularly soggy ground then, assuming there is sensible agreement, you may drop at the nearest point of relief away from that particular area using the point of entry as your reference. And, the lord be praised, that is about it.

RULE 26...WATER HAZARDS

OH DEAR, water hazards are to the game of golf what a blizzard is to tennis: they definitely complicate things. So, from the top, what exactly constitutes a water hazard? Well, officially, it is any sea, lake, pond, river, ditch, surface drainage ditch, or other type of open water course. Sometimes it does not even have to actually contain any water. For example, drainage ditches, by their very nature, are often dry. Then there are two types of water hazards. There is your straightforward water hazard and there is your lateral water hazard.

The straightforward water hazards may be identified by the color of the stakes and lines marking the perimeters of the hazard. These will be yellow, while a lateral hazard will be identified by red markings. The essential difference between the two is that you can easily gain access to the rear of a water hazard, while a lateral tends to run alongside the fairway and so it would be impractical, if not impossible, to stand behind it and thus keep the water between yourself and the hole.

COFFEE BREAK

SOMETIMES even journalists have their uses on the golf circuit. A classic example of this came in the 1960s during the Canada Cup match at St. Nom-la-Breteche, a delightful course just outside Paris, France. The drama involved Mark Wilson, who was then writing about golf for the London Evening Standard, *and legendary Irish golfer Christy O'Connor Senior, or "Himself" as his army of admirers knew him.*

When Wilson bumped into O'Connor on his way to the tee on the first morning he noted that his friend was wearing a distinctly bleary look. Explained Wilson: "It had been a very, very good night at the Irish Embassy the evening before and Christy, as ever, had been entertained to excess. When I saw him that morning he clearly was not very well. Unfortunately he was already hurrying to the tee without the benefit of breakfast so when he saw me he croaked, 'Wilson, fetch me a pot of black coffee.' I told him that I couldn't bring a pot of coffee on to the first tee in the Canada Cup.

"Instead I offered to stand to the side of the first fairway, round about where his opening drive should land. In order to maintain discretion I actually stood back among the trees so none of the spectators could see me. Christy, however, did and he deliberately sliced his drive into the trees right alongside me. He walked in, took a look at his ball, grinned at me, gulped the coffee, clipped his ball out, and went on to play a marvelous round. Tremendous man."

WATER HAZARDS
The different coloured stakes:
- **Yellow stakes — water hazard**
  Identify the point your ball crossed the hazard and drop as far back as you like in line with the flag, under penalty of one stroke.
- **Red stakes — lateral water hazard**
  Identify the point your ball entered the hazard and drop within two club lengths of this point or a corresponding point on the other side of the hazard.

If your ball enters a water hazard—and you should have reasonable evidence of this fact—then you have three options. First, you may play it as you find it, although this is rarely advisable (ask Jean Van de Velde why not). Sometimes the ball will be within the lines of the hazard but will have stayed out of the water itself so obviously you just hit it but remember not to ground your club.

The second option is to play a ball from behind the water hazard, having first defined where the ball actually crossed the line of the hazard and keeping this spot between you and the flag. You may retreat as far as you like if you do this. The penalty is one shot. If you wish you may return to the spot from which you first struck the ball into the hazard and play again, thus losing a stroke and forfeiting the distance.

These options also apply to a lateral hazard but now you may also define the point at which your ball first crossed the line of the hazard and drop within two club lengths with the added bonus that you may draw a line from here to the opposite side of the water—usually a ditch—and play from there in the same manner of dropping and under the same penalty of a shot. Okay? Good, let's get out of here.

RULE 27...LOST BALL

FINDING BALLS is fun. Losing them is not. A ball is deemed lost if you and your playing partner(s) have spent five minutes looking for it and failed. At this point even if it is found, it is lost, if you see what I mean. I often feel there is an element of unfairness here compared to what happens at, say, The Open Championship where upwards of 200 people often look for a player's ball whereas the most I've ever had is four. Now 200 x five minutes = MORE THAN 16 HOURS! Ah well, just thought I'd mention it.

As you know, having read the earlier rule, if your ball is lost in abnormal ground (disappeared into a muddy mess that used to be a fairway most likely) then you may drop another one without penalty. And any time you fear you may have lost a ball, play a provisional as this helps to speed up play and anything that does this gets my vote every time. There is an exception … you can't bring a provisional into play if you think you've lost the ball in a water hazard.

If you suspect your ball may be lost then you may play a provisional—first having clearly announced the fact to another player—and you may continue to play this until you reach the place where your first ball may be. If you find it, then you pocket the provisional and carry on, but if you hit the provisional from a point that turns out to be either even with or ahead of your original ball, then the second ball becomes the "ball in play" and no amount of foot stamping will remedy this unnecessary situation or cancel the one-shot penalty you have now incurred.

RULE 28...BALL UNPLAYABLE

ONLY YOU can decide when your ball is unplayable. For you it may be, for Tiger Woods on the other hand it may not. Only you can judge your own ability—or perhaps lack of ability—in any given situation. Once decided, however, you have three clear options.

OPTION 1:
- You may return to the spot from which the ball was originally struck and shake hands with our old friend 'stroke and distance'.

OPTION 2:
- Under a one shot penalty you may drop a ball

within two club lengths of where the ball has
been declared unplayable. Use your driver to
do this and mark the optimum spot with a tee
peg before dropping not nearer the hole.

OPTION 3:

* If, say, the ball is in a bush or similar then
draw an imaginary line from the flag to your
ball and then drop it behind this bush. You
may go back as far as you like but wherever
you drop it you do so under a one shot penalty.

Each of these options is available to you if you are in
a hazard except that with regard to Options 2 and 3 you
must drop the ball inside the hazard. If this is a bunker
then any drop is likely to encourage at least a semiburied
lie so be careful.

Finally, the only place on a golf course where you
may not ever declare a ball unplayable is—you've guessed
it —when it is in a water hazard. There really is something
to be said for desert golf courses …

Hole	Rating/Slope	1	2	3	4	5	6
Black	73.1/140	526	472	197	313	157	403
Blue	70.3/131	504	419	182	292	136	375
White	68.7/123	480	393	160	268	115	349
Men's Hdcp		7	1	9	13	17	15
		6	5	4	6	5	
		2	1		2	3	
		5	4	3	4	3	

GOLF GAMES

| | | | 242 | 105 | 330 | 120 |
| | | | | | | |

GIVE a man a set of clubs and a bit of time to think about it and he will come up with the most outlandish ways of playing golf for fun, for money, for titles or, most importantly, for some respite from the dull cares of general life. The boundaries for this exercise are limitless, defined only by your own imagination—or somebody else's. The basic fact is that golf is a game, it's there to promote enjoyment, and how you enjoy it is up to you, your pals, and the laws of decency prevailing at the time.

There is always a lot of talk about the "spirit of the game" and often this chatter can droop into the most sappy and irritatingly pretentious drivel, however well meant. Let's cut to the chase here. For me, the spirit of the game is captured perfectly on a toilet wall at Shinnecock Hills Golf Club. I first went to Shinnecock in the mid '80s to cover the U.S. Open. It was love at first sight. The course, set in the Hamptons outside New York, is a spectacular links; the white clapboard clubhouse designed by Stanford White is one of the oldest in North America. It is, however, without doubt the prettiest I have seen and it was here that I also first saw the two framed quotes hanging either side of a basin in the men's room. The one on the left said: "Some people like great art or classical music but for me the most wonderful sight in the world is of a white golf ball arcing against an azure blue sky." It was signed "Arnold Palmer, Latrobe, Pennsylvania, 1969." I thought, "Aaahh, bless."

Then I glanced to my right. Here, the framed quote read: "Give me a sunny day, a set of golf clubs, and a beautiful woman and you can keep the golf clubs." This one was signed "Jack Benny, Los Angeles, 1968." And I thought "Thank God." Here in these two quotes—one from the most charismatic American golfer ever and the other from one of the truly great and original wits this varied land has yet produced—was, it seems to me, something of the real spirit of the game. On one hand golf encourages a serious application of the senses on top of a rare focus if it is to be played anything near well, but on the other it does not matter a damn. It is the gloriously significant but trivially unimportant twin aspects of the grand old game that bring me back to it constantly. I hope you feel the same.

Now, shall we play?

THE CLASSIC FORMS OF GOLF

THERE are two classic bedrocks of the game, stroke play (sometimes called medal play) and match play. Somehow as the 20th century meandered on its chaotic and confused way, stroke play, recording the total number of shots played

LEARNING TO WIN

LEE TREVINO learned early that having the nerve to play golf for money counted almost as much as actual talent for hitting the ball. Trevino found out because, as a poor kid growing up on the Tex-Mex border in El Paso, he made most of his pay gambling at golf.

As a teenager he worked as a handyman at Horizon Hills, a club high on a dusty hill, mostly populated by local cotton farmers who always played for serious dollar bills. Trevino was often bankrolled by these members to play money matches against other young Texan golfers and so one day a match was set up against Raymond Floyd.

Floyd was already on the PGA Tour but he loved to play dollar matches and his friends loved to back him. When Floyd arrived at the club, Lee greeted him, carried his clubs into the lockerroom and looked after him. Eventually Floyd asked if Trevino knew who he was playing that afternoon. "Me," said Trevino. Floyd then retreated for lunch and passed up the chance to have an early look at the course, saying he had met his opponent and preparation was not necessary.

Typically, Floyd overpowered Horizon Hills to post a 67 that day. Everyone was impressed. But they were more impressed by Trevino who shot 65 to win. Lots of money changed hands. Trevino felt rich. Floyd felt irritated. The next time Floyd saw Trevino he was joining in the applause as Lee won the U.S. Open in 1968. "Man, playing those money games taught me how to win. Learning how to win is different again from learning how to play," he reflected.

over 18 holes, gained the upper hand in golf, establishing itself as the premier method of determining who was a champion golfer and who was not. The four major championships—the Masters and U.S. Open, The British Open, and the Championship PGA—all rely on stroke play over 72 holes. The reasons for this preeminence, in the professional game at least, is partly because the professionals prefer it and they prefer it because luck, good, bad or indifferent, tends to balance itself out over four days of golf with the emphasis on how you perform rather than how your opponents play.

This, they say, is the best test of skill. And so it is, but the other reason for the prevalence of this type of card-and-pencil golf is because in the second half of the 20th century the television people let it be known it was what they liked too. Stroke play is much easier for the TV scheduler to, well, schedule, whereas match play—playing an opponent hole by hole—can end early or stumble on late. It is more than a small pity, however, that there is so little match play at the highest levels of the game and no accident that one of the most popular and exciting competitions available to the paying public is the Ryder Cup, which is, of course, entirely match play. The irony here is that these same TV companies are willing to pay many millions of dollars to broadcast it. Yet it is match play that forms the cornerstone of the way most amateurs play the game. The reasons here are simple enough to grasp. Whereas in stroke play an entire round can be ruined because some atrocious luck allied to serious incompetence on an early hole means a player running up a score that can screech into double figures before you can say "shucks," match play offers triumph and disaster in equal measure. In other words, by playing the man (your opponent) rather than the course, your score at each hole does not matter except inasmuch as it dictates whether you have won, lost, or halved the thing. If you take an eleven (shucks! again) but Fred takes twelve then, hurrah, you've won the hole. No one ever asks you how many strokes you took after a match play round or at least they shouldn't. All that counts is whether you won, lost, or halved the match. Best of all you do not need a pencil to write down scores after each hole, although quite often it is advisable to do so in order to avoid any confusion as to the state of the match at any given point. This optional chore becomes mandatory once over the age of 55, by which time merely trying to remember your opponent's name encourages a panic attack. At least, as best I recall it does.

Match play also offers up the opportunity for actually reacting to what an opponent is doing. If, for example, he is busy somewhere in the trees having sliced his drive wildly, then, if you are on the fairway, consider the safest, most dependable shot you may now play that will encourage your ball toward the green. There is nothing worse than going for it when you don't have to and then finding a dog of a lie to the side of the green, which means instead of winning a hole easily you end up halving it or worse. The other rule of life affecting match play is this: GET ON WITH IT. If you are "out" of a hole, concede it and move on. Don't mess about and don't ever say, "If you don't mind I'll play this hole out because I want to keep a total score." At least don't say it to me. Or most people of my acquaintance.

So that is stroke play and match play. The first means every stroke counts over 18 holes and the second means only the hole score counts. I know which version of the game I prefer. As that great Irish amateur Joe Carr once remarked, "Stroke play is a better test of golf but match play is a better test of character." Quite so, although Joe could have added "and provider of fun."

FUN GAMES & VARIATIONS

MATCH PLAY and stoke play are not the be-all and end-all of the game. Why not try out some of these fun variations to spice up your Sunday foursome?

STABLEFORD

THE FIRST and most popular variation to stroke or match play golf is Stableford. This is to say that you utilize the

Stableford system of scoring invented in 1931 thanks to the fertile imagination of Dr. Frank Stableford, who played his golf at Wallasey on Merseyside, England, and who began his medical career as a surgeon in the Boer War. There is, to be fair, some serious dispute about this as it was discovered in 1990 that a Dr. F. Stableford also had been a member of Glamorganshire Golf Club in South Wales some 30 years earlier and a similar system had been utilized there as early as 1898. Whatever the real facts here the relevant point remains that the good doctor's genius means that the game may be played in a stroke-play fashion but happily minus the "shucks" factor. This is because points are awarded, or at least are available to be awarded, on each hole depending on your score. The assigned par score on each hole is worth two points; a bogey (one over par) is worth one. Pull off a birdie (one under par) and you earn three points, an eagle (two under par) brings in four points, and if you ever pick up five points then you've done incandescently better than I've ever managed. This game may be played off either full handicap or an agreed percentage of that handicap, but for the sake of argument and by way of explanation let us assume you have an 18 handicap and that your Stableford game is to be played off full handicap. This means you will have a shot on each hole. So if you achieve par without using your "shot" then you subtract one stroke and end up with a birdie, which in turn is worth three points. This also means that you may double bogey (two shots over par) a hole and still earn a point. A return in the low 30s represents a reasonable performance, while 36 points means you have played exactly to your handicap. A score of 40 or more points suggests either you have enjoyed one of those glorious days that are sent as a happy contrast to the norm, or that your handicap needs a serious looking at. The rather unsettling fact is that when the doc invented the Stableford system of scoring he also preset the conditions for the golfing bandit to emerge. But that's life, not golf. Rise above it. It won't happen often.

FOURSOMES

NO ONE knows who invented foursomes golf but the first written record of it that I've unearthed was by H. B. Farnie in *The Golfer's Manual* published in 1857. However, whoever came up with this idea of two players combining to compete against another pair, each duo playing one ball by alternate strokes, had an exceptionally polished and impish sense of humor. Few moments in the game compare with that which can often arise in foursomes play. Imagine that you have just thumped a drive as far as you can and down the middle of a fairway. Now it's your partner's turn to hit the next shot. The ball is lying wonderfully well, the green appears as welcoming as a happy bartender's smile on a winter's evening, everything is so absolutely pristine that you would welcome the opportunity to hit this approach yourself.

But you can't. Instead you must watch your partner, quite probably your close friend, take on the modest challenge of PUTTING THE BLOODY THING ON THE GREEN. And, naturally, often he doesn't. Instead he tops it sideways and into the swamp. "Sorry," he mumbles, head down in embarrassment. "There's no need to say sorry," you reply in time-honored fashion while thinking, "Something in writing accompanied by a bottle or two would be much more flaming appropriate to the shambles you've just made of probably the finest drive I have ever hit at this hole."

Welcome to the charm, the challenge, and above all the exquisite fun of foursomes golf. Usually, but not necessarily, played under a match-play format, foursomes combines camaraderie, closeness, and sometimes even love with a bitter feeling of regret that you are, on this particular day, tied irretrievably to an incompetent turd. Taken in the right spirit this only adds to the charm of foursomes play.

One small but vital point to end on… the order in which you play is decided by you and your partner. Essentially this means you occupy the tee on either the odd or the even holes. It doesn't matter who actually holed out, the order must be kept when you move on to the next tee. Oh, and it is advisable to work out in which order the short holes occur. Usually, but by no means always, there are four par 3s per 18 holes and often three of these will either be off

THE ROYAL & ANCIENT

THE R&A clubhouse at St. Andrews, Scotland, was built in 1854 and is reassuringly stern—four walls built to withstand the worst that the North Sea can throw at it. In a changing world this squat building accurately reflects the unwavering commitment of the Royal & Ancient Golf Club to golf's core values.

While the exterior is forbidding, the interior is reassuringly warm and welcoming. The wood-paneled reception area is the sort that suggests class, money, and a concern for aesthetics.

From there one may wander into the Big Room—or lounge to you and me—the ceiling dominated by a magnificent chandelier, the walls festooned with near priceless paintings, each depicting either a golf scene or a significant character.

There are many millions of pounds worth of golf treasures inside this fortress, but it is the sight of The Open Championship Trophy, the elegant claret jug raised triumphantly aloft each year by the champion, that attracts visitors to this special house, where they may gaze at it in a glass cabinet.

Yes, the one the champ gets is a replica, a decision made by the committee in 1927. But because the two are identical, five-time Open winner Tom Watson was once presented with the original by mistake. Fortunately this error was discovered the following year when the trophy needed to have a small dent repaired and the original 1873 hallmark was noticed. Phew!

odd or even-numbered tees. If one of you is a relatively superior striker of the ball, especially with long or medium-iron shots, then this is the player who should endeavor to take on these short holes. "Think on!" as they used to say at one of my old clubs, Glossop in Derbyshire, England. And "think on" we did. Sometimes.

GREENSOMES

GREENSOMES is good fun to play and, as it's a strictly unofficial form of the grand old game, you can tweak around with it to your heart's content. Usually this game is played in groups of four and by a pair of golfers against another pair. Essentially it is foursomes but with the added bonus that BOTH players hit drives. You then choose which ball to play and from there on in it's alternate shots as in foursomes. What may be added to inject a further frisson of drama to the game is that each player MUST hit a nominated number of drives. This may be, for example, six drives, and what it means is that if one of you is a particularly long and accurate driver of the ball the other partner cannot relax because one in three drives must be his. Choosing which of these often inferior drives to take adds a delicious complication to the whole affair.

GRUESOMES

IN THIS mad variant of the rather tame Greensomes, the

great difference is that your opponents get to choose which drive you have to hit and, unless they are graduates of the Not Very Smart School of Thought, then naturally they will choose the drive that has ended in the rough or found a hazard. Except that sometimes this means the superior player on the other side gets to play the ball and that may rebound nastily. As an exercise in reverse psychology Gruesomes is often without peer.

YELLOWSOMES

ANOTHER variant of Greensomes, which for some is a step too far. In this game you have a partner and you each hit a ball off the tee but the twist here is that you each now must play from the position of the worst shot. This may mean merely conceding a few yards in distance or it may mean playing from behind a tree or out of a hazard. Then the next-worst shot must be played and so on until the ball is in the hole. As an exercise in futility this game is without peer but it can be a bit of fun as well, although it should never be played unless the course is particularly quiet. I recommend you try it once. You'll be unlikely to try it again.

FOUR BALL

ONE of the most popular forms of play, this match play game involves, guess what, four players, two versus two. You play your own ball and the lowest net score on a hole counts for that pair against their opponent's score. The way in which handicaps are applied can be decided on the first tee but, for me, the best way to do this is for the low man to become scratch and for the other three to then have three-quarters of the difference in their actual handicaps. So… your four ball has an 8 handicapper, a 10, a 15, and an 18. Subtract 8 from the other three handicaps and you are left with 2, 7, and 11, which under the three-quarters system means that these players respectively receive two, five, and eight strokes against the 8 handicapper who is now playing off scratch. Don't fret, it works.

ROUND ROBIN

SAME as four ball but even more sociable as each player pairs up with a different partner from the group over six holes. Decide who starts with whom by tossing coins or lobbing the contestants' four balls in the air and whichever two land closest together starts as a pairing. This may mean Tom playing with Dick over the first six holes, then Tom partnering Harry over the middle six and ending up with Fred over the final half dozen. Holes are won, drawn, or halved as usual—obviously one pair may lose a hole while the other two pairs halve it—and points are awarded for a win or a half-point for a half. By this method you have three matches within the 18 holes and then an overall winner (or winners). Points can be turned into cash or drinks although if the latter is chosen make sure you are not driving. Better still, play a few matches and have a night out.

LIMITED CLUBS

SELF-EXPLANATORY really. Instead of hauling 14 clubs out on to the course as per usual and not using at least half of them, limit yourself and your playing partners to a specified number of clubs. This number is up to yourselves or the overall organizer if this is a group outing, but the most amusement I've ever enjoyed has been when three clubs has been the limit. Sometimes one of these is nominated as a putter but this does not always have to be the case as, for example, a 2- or 3- iron can be an effective "putter." Ben Crenshaw discovered this in 1987 during the Ryder Cup when he suffered a fit of bad temper and smacked his putter against the ground, and the head snapped off. Crenshaw had to use his 2-iron over the remaining half-dozen holes against Ireland's Eamonn Darcy. This he did effectively, but not effectively enough to defeat Darcy and the United States went on to lose for the first time on home soil.

Anyway, whichever clubs you choose you will, I promise, be amazed at how well you can score with just a few of your usual weapons. Apart from taking away the confusing chore of choosing from 14 of these babies, finding different ways to use, say, a 5-iron will swiftly improve your shot-making skill and your ability to visualize a shot.

AUGUSTA BURNING

For the first 15 years of my Masters odyssey the clubhouse bar was run brilliantly by a large, African American guy who went by the name of Arthur. He was an impressive figure. Quietly spoken but hugely authoritative, Arthur became a friend as well as a supplier of especially fine white wine.

One year during my visit I went to see the powerful film Mississippi Burning *which illuminates an ugly chapter in American history, revealing the appalling array of white supremacist atrocities that took place in the Deep South. The next day I—as a visiting Brit— asked Arthur what it had been like growing up in a segregated Augusta, Georgia, in the 1940s.*

He took my hand, looked at me for several long seconds and said "Mr Elliott" (he would never call me Bill) "you don't wanna know, sir." In reply I told him that his eyes had just told me everything I needed to know.

Arthur retired a couple of years before Tiger Woods won his first Masters in 1997 but I thought of him as I watched the only presentation ceremony I've ever bothered to attend. A few yards away two young, black, very happy waiters were high-fiving each other as the blazer was draped over an equally young Woods while Lee Elder, the first black golfer to play in the Masters was in tears. Wherever Arthur was that day I hoped that he realized the world, especially Augusta, had moved forward—a bit anyway.

Remember that Seve Ballesteros taught himself how to play some of the most imaginative and creative golf in history because the only club he had to practice with as a youngster in Spain a was a cut-down 3-iron that his brother Manuel gave him. Years later I watched during a U.S. Open as Jack Nicklaus nominated shots for Seve to play out of a practice bunker with his 3-iron. After watching Ballesteros hit the ball long, short, high, and low to order out of the sand, Nicklaus walked away smiling and shaking his head in wonder.

PICK UP STICKS

PERSONALLY I call this game Nick a Stick. It's a form of match play but with the added bonus—or should this be minus?—that when you lose a hole you may take one club in your opponent's bag out of play. This club may be reclaimed when your opponent loses a hole at which point he may nick one of yours. Half handicaps should be used in this game although this is arbitrary. One thing you need to decide beforehand is whether the putter is liable to confiscation. There is a school of thought that believes it is too much of a handicap not to have a putter but, hey, the whole idea of this game is a basic, and entirely satisfying, unfairness so why not? As a variation on this variation you may also decide that the higher handicap player may, off the bat, remove one club from his opponent's bag for every two-stroke difference in their handicaps. Say this is eight shots—a 10 handicapper playing an 18—then four clubs may be deemed out of play on the first tee although these may be reclaimed as holes are won. IF holes are won. By the way don't always go for the opposition driver, as this is often the club that gets them into trouble in the first place. "Think on!" once again.

NINE POINT

SO CALLED because nine points are available on each hole. Although it can be played by three golfers it is better played by four. The winning score on each hole is awarded five points, the next best score gets three, the next is awarded one point, while the highest score on the hole receives zero. If two players tie for the lowest score—net of handicap of course—then they get four points each while if everyone scores the same then each receives two and a quarter points. The guy with the highest number of points at the end is the winner, naturally. If you are a three ball then play as above but simply remove the zero point option so that five, three, and one points are available on each hole.

CROSS COUNTRY

BE WARNED, not all clubs approve of this game and in any case it should never be attempted except on those happy occasions when you and a few pals find yourselves on an empty track. It's usually best to play the first hole as it lies.

Whoever wins this hole may choose the next hole but this will not be a hole off the card or anything that the architect intended. Instead choose to play from whichever tee to a different hole. So you might play from the second tee to the fifth green and so on. It all depends on the layout of the course you are playing. Some courses lend themselves to this more than others but if you manage to play it then you will experience the thrill of being your own architect for a while and it can revitalize interest in a home course that has grown rather jaded because of your familiarity with its features.

THREE-PLAYER GAMES

PLAYING the game as a threesome is recommended. Firstly, it is perhaps the most convivial form of a game that always should err on the side of being seriously sociable and, secondly, it means that if you are playing with a particularly morose individual whose wife has just slipped away with the grocer's delivery boy (or girl) then you may ignore him and chat away with the third member of the group.

Most crucially, however, it is a much quicker way of playing golf than the four ball. Of course logic dictates that it should indeed be 25 percent quicker but in reality it is swifter than this. Quite why this should be has confounded some of the finest mathematical minds of several generations but there you are, it just is.

There are lots of games for the trio to play and from these I have extracted five for you to contemplate.

THREE BALL

IN THIS form of golf each player takes on the other two in separate matches. Handicaps, of course, have to be carefully deciphered so as to make it fair on everyone. The fun comes for two reasons. Firstly, one may savor the ultimate joy of beating both the other players but, secondly, even if down in one match there may always be the possibility of success in the other and a subsequent saving of both face and pocket. On the other hand...

THREESOME

THIS GAME used to be hugely popular but now, rather sadly, seems to be as rare as a double eagle. It shouldn't be because it offers a most enjoyable method by which two higher handicap players may—just may—bring down a far superior golfer. Anyway, in threesome play one golfer takes on the other two. The twist is that the paired side play alternate shots. Foursome golf if you like—except that it is threesome.

SIX POINT

THIS is a popular form of play in the United States where it is more commonly known as "English." Why? I've no idea.

BOTTLE ... AND HOW TO USE ONE

MAKING money from professional golf happens in a variety of ways. The most obvious is the prize money but, huge though this revenue is from the modern game, it is almost small change to the superstars whose endorsements make them many more millions than they ever win in a tournament.

The godfather of this sort of personal sponsorship was Mark McCormack. Big Mac died a couple of years ago but he will be remembered as both a decent guy and the man who transformed, first, golf and then almost every other game thanks to his imagination and financial acumen. I first saw just how good he was at what he did immediately after Tony Jacklin won his British Open title at Royal Lytham & St Annes in 1969. A gaggle of photographers wanted a special celebratory picture of the new, young, English champ and so they clubbed together and bought a bottle of the finest Moet & Chandon champagne, gave it to Tony, and told him to pose with it. Jacklin was happy to oblige and as he stood there with the bottle to his lips the snappers prepared to shoot.

Suddenly McCormack walked up to Jacko, whispered something to him, and turned the bottle around so the label was not in shot. Later, I asked Tony what he had said. He explained: "He told me we hadn't done a deal with the champagne company. Yet. And so we shouldn't be giving them any free publicity." One sharp man was Mark McCormack.

Anyway, to the point—or rather six of them. These points are available on each hole and may be split in various ways. You may award four points to the lowest score and two to the next lowest with zero going to the third player. Or the two players with the lowest scores get three points each and the last man again gets zip. Or the player with the lowest score picks up four points and the other two get a point each no matter what they score. It all depends how fair/unfair/generally crotchety you feel on the day.

CHAIRMAN

THIS REALLY is an enjoyable way of playing three ball golf. Here the first person to win a hole outright becomes the Chairman. Each hole he then wins as Chairman counts for one unit, or point. You can only win a unit while you are the Chairman, remember. If the Chairman halves a hole with another player then no units are distributed but he remains in the chair. Played off handicap this is a most equitable form of play and one that rewards consistently decent golf, although it is difficult both to attain the chair and then to win a hole while sitting in this position of power.

WOLF

PLAYED off full handicap, Wolf is a game of intrigue and shenanigans for three players. A player becomes the Wolf by hitting the middle distance drive off the tee no matter where the ball has landed, fairway, rough, or deepest divot. If it is a par 3 then it is the second nearest ball that gets to cry Wolf while the other two players become the Hunters. The Wolf must then double his net score on this hole and match it against the combined net score of his two opponents. If the amount wagered on each hole is, say, a dollar per person (it could be a penny but then would it be worth the effort?) then the Wolf, if he wins, picks up two bucks from the others. If he loses he pays them a dollar each and if the hole is halved then, usually, the stake is carried forward, and thus doubled, for the next hole and so on until someone wins. Strategy off the tee becomes important because only by being the Wolf can you win the big pots—although obviously you can also lose them—and so players jockey for position trying to become the second longest off the tee. In this way the longer hitters are not as advantaged as they might be under normal circumstances.

GAMES FOR SINGLETONS

WE ALL GO solo from time to time whether by choice, if we are feeling particularly unsociable, or because a playing partner has called in sick (although he'd better be on death's door to have let me down). Either way, some of the most enjoyable times to be had on a course are when you are playing golf on your own and have the opportunity to develop a deep focus on top of the chance to reflect on life, the universe and a couple of other things. And at least this way you get to play with someone you really, really like. And you win every time. Even if you lose, if you see what I mean.

MATCH PLAY AGAINST PAR

USING your full handicap, take on the par for each hole. Do not cheat, do not give yourself a putt, do not award yourself another shot. Count EVERYTHING and see how you do. If you manage to beat Mr. Par fairly and squarely then your game is improving. More importantly, your ability to concentrate properly while playing golf is improving too. In the end, we all play golf by ourselves. Even if we are in the midst of a significant competition, golf is a solitary game, played within our minds. Playing on your own, practicing on your own, is the best way to improve. Certainly it is how the very finest players on the planet practice. Those other practice sessions with a couple of other professionals are just for show as well as, almost certainly, a little dough.

TWO BALL SOLO

UNLESS the course is unusually quiet, life as a singleton can be fairly dreary. Until recently, as a single player you had no standing in golf so that the group of four laboring fools ahead of you had no requirement to let you through. It is a constant source of sad astonishment to me how many golfers allowed this fact to override what would be normal courtesy and so they, sometimes rather pointedly, ignored your presence behind them. Since the sensible change by the rulemakers, it is the pace of play alone that is supposed to dictate priority on the course, but it is inevitable that as a singleton for one reason or another you will have to wait around. One way to alleviate this situation is to play two balls off each tee, one ball against the other. Again, no cheating, no letting up on yourself. Hit the balls, find them, and hit them again from wherever they lie. On some holes hit one with a driver and one with a shorter club that is more or less guaranteed to keep this ball in play. See which ball wins. And remember the strategy used the next time you play this hole. Sometimes discretion can be the key to heady success in this most perverse of games. The fact is that playing by yourself can prepare you well to beat others. It will also teach you patience. Or it should. And you don't have to buy a round when you get back to the clubhouse. If this is a good thing.

THE LAST HURRAH

JACK Nicklaus's 18th, and last, Major victory came at the 1986 Masters. At 46, he should not have been a contender. And he wasn't until he sliced his drive into trees at the eighth hole during the final round on Sunday.

For once the great strategist threw caution to the wind, handed a 7-iron back to his son who was caddying for him, and selected a wood instead.

By chance I happened to be one of just a dozen or so people watching him at the time (there are now several thousand apparently) and so I was able to marvel at the shot he produced, his ball soaring through a gap so small it would have challenged even a daringly acrobatic squirrel. He saved his par at that hole and suddenly Jack was young again and the birdies flowed over the remaining holes. Leader Seve Ballesteros folded under the pressure pouring off the older maestro, and an extraordinary victory was constructed.

It was the finest Major victory I think I can safely say I have ever witnessed—a sporting sensation that enthused just about everyone. Especially middle-aged men all over the planet who fell out of bed the next day with renewed vigor. Some even managed to go to bed with fresh enthusiasm.

GAMBLING GAMES

YOU DO NOT have to play golf for money. On the other hand you do not need to eat caviar and champagne to survive this challenging life but, let us agree right now, the occasional splurge does the soul good. Sir Henry Cotton taught me very early that playing the grand old game for a few pounds added a little spice and turned what might have been merely an enjoyable meander around the course into something greater, a real test of swing, of character, and ultimately of nerve.

Indeed dear Henry's dictum was precise: "Always play for money, old boy," he told me all those years ago. "And furthermore always play for a little more than you would care to lose. In this way you will concentrate on the job in hand and thus will your golf improve. To succeed at golf a player must learn how to move out of his, or her, comfort zone. Pressure, in this case encouraged by betting, is the secret to progress in my opinion." Henry, of course, won three Opens and much besides.

SKINS

SO, having established that a wager is as good a lesson as any for the golfer—and often better—let us glance at one of the most popular forms of gambling, the Skins game.

If you are struggling to put shoes on the children's feet, worried about the making the next mortgage payment, or otherwise financially stretched then, unless you are a particularly free spirit, I suggest you read about a Skins match and then forget it. Skins, like free-fall parachuting or finger climbing in the French Alps, is exhilarating and it is exhilarating because it is dangerous.

The basic rules are simple although the prerequisite number of players is set in stone, for this is a game for three or four players. Or more if your club allows a bit of freedom on a late summer's evening. First you decide on how much a skin should be worth. This may be a few cents—but why bother?— or a dollar or, if you are Tiger, a few hundred dollars. This skin is then available at each hole.

It is only won if one player wins that hole. If two halve the hole then the third—and/or fourth—player loses nothing because that skin is then carried on to the next hole where two skins are available. Unlikely though it is, it may transpire that no hole is won outright through the first 17 and so all 18 skins are available on the last. If, say, you were part of a four ball playing for a one-dollar skin then $72 would be in the pot by this point. If you then win outright at the 18th you will net $54 ($72 minus your own input, which would be $18). This rarely happens of course but, whatever the initial skin is worth, always multiply it by 18 because this then is your total potential loss.

This may to some brittle souls seem rather daunting. If so, do what I do, and multiply it by 54 because this is your

YOU WANNA BET?

GOLF used to be full of real characters. Players like the inseparable northern England professionals Hedley Muscroft and Lionel Platts. This larger-than-life double act reckoned they were pretty much unbeatable as a team and used to make a lot of money from taking on gullible amateurs with more money than sense. Even on the rare occasion that they lost one of these games they usually had some scam aimed at getting back their money—and a profit—in the bar afterwards.

In a classic example of their ingenuity they once turned the tables on a couple of Americans who had beaten them. This was upsetting, of course, but Muscroft and Platts were even more upset by their opponents' rather overbearing attitude and determined to bring them down a peg or two.

Over a drink Hedley suddenly pointed to the grassy incline outside the clubhouse window. "See that hill, pal," he said. "I bet you fifty bucks that I can carry Lionel up and down that before you can drink a pint of water."

The bet was accepted and, while everyone gathered outside to see what happened, Hedley went off to order the water. Once outside he gathered Lionel onto his back and then the waiter appeared with the pint. Unfortunately for the Americans the water had just been boiled.

potential maximum upside to the deal. When gambling at golf it pays to be an eternal optimist. Arnold Palmer has always been an optimist and in 1990 during the annual Skins Game created by ABC Television he won more money on one hole—several hundred thousand dollars—than he had ever won in any one year as a pro. It is also worth noting that this TV show pulls in more viewers than any other golf outside the Masters in the States. Watching rich people become even richer really is a spectator sport.

NASSAU

THIS REALLY is the universal gambling game of choice. All my golfing life I have assumed this gamble originated in the Bahamas but now I know that it started a century ago at the Nassau Country Club, which turns out to be on Long Island, New York. I'd have lost a lot of money betting against this fact but there you have it. Anyway, the story goes that in around 1900 this golf club could boast a formidable team, so formidable they rarely lost to opponents. So, in an effort to try to inject some drama into their effortless victories, someone came up with dividing the match into three parts, the front nine, the back nine, and the overall match with a point available for each segment. Nowadays it is money rather than points that is used and so if someone says to you "Five, five, and five?" on the first tee they are offering you a Nassau bet with five dollars up for grabs over the first nine holes, five on the back, and then a final

five on the result of the match. Obviously this means that
if you win the front 2&1 but lose the back nine 3&2 then
you have lost overall. Your five won on the first nine is
canceled out by the money lost on the back and so you have
to cough up five bucks for the match result. In what passes
as polite society for me, the assumption always is that the
match result should be worth double either of the nines so
if you played me it would not be "Five, five, and five?" but
"Five, five, and ten?" with a ten going to the match victors.
If there are any.

Nassau is particularly good for a four ball pairs match
but it can be used for two balls as well. The amount wagered
is up to you, your opponents, and everyone's current fiscal
state. Some golfers play for pennies, others for thousands.
That's your call. And you should be aware that this Nassau
game also offers up the chance of presses. A press can come
when the back nine is won with a few holes left. It can only
be requested by the losing side—although it does not have to
be called—and it need not be accepted by the winners
although it is considered appalling to decline. And I do
mean REALLY appalling. The press is always for the same
amount as has just been lost. So if you've lost five dollars on
the front and you press over the remaining, say, two holes
then you are playing for another five dollars over this stretch.
You may even "press the press" if you then lose that. This
can get complicated and is therefore only recommended for

Nassau veterans or if you are playing with an Emeritus
Professor of Mathematics.

BINGO BANGO BONGO

I'VE GOT no idea where the name for this game comes
from although I do have a sneaking suspicion it is more
likely to be Colonial Africa than Yorkshire or anywhere else
in the British Isles or the United States. Certainly it's worth
playing if only so you may say the name out loud and alarm
everyone on the first tee. More seriously, it is an effective
game when you have a spread of handicaps playing together
in a group of four.

There are three points available on each hole—that's the
bingo, the bango, and the bongo—and so it's a format that
puts a separate points value on the long game, short game,
and putting. The first point is awarded to the player hitting
the green in the fewest shots (fringes don't count and ties get
a half point each by the way), the second goes to the player
closest to the hole after everyone is on the green, and this is
regardless of how many strokes it has taken to get there so
there is always something to play for. And the third point
goes to whoever is down in the fewest strokes. Handicaps,
if used at all, only apply to this final point.

On short holes there is a twist to all this inasmuch as
the first point goes to the player who is second closest to the
hole after everyone is on the green. The beauty of this format

is that it may reward players of varying abilities and usually there is something to play for no matter how poorly you may have started a hole.

SNAKE

THIS GAME goes under various guises but in the States, where it is most popular, it is called Snake. It's a game within the game because it focuses on putting. The first player to three-putt is the snake and remains so until someone else three-putts (or worse) unless he three-stabs himself at the same time. Then it is the player holding the snake at the end of the ninth and 18th holes who must pay the others an agreed amount. Of course, this may be the first time this hapless individual has been the snake but that's half the fun and you would be surprised how often this slippery creature changes names on those two greens. This, may I remind you, is because of pressure, and learning to handle this baleful-eyed beast is at least half the reason we play these games in the first place.

LONE WOLF

A SERIOUS gambling game, Lone Wolf is also a serious exercise in psychology, bluffology, and almost every other ology you can muster. Designed for four golfers, one player is designated Wolf on the first tee and hits first. He then has a choice. He may pick a partner and play against the

IT'S ONLY MONEY AFTER ALL

NOWADAYS the top golfers never actually see the money they win. Instead their management company takes care of all this fussy, financial detail. Platoons of accountants deal with everything so that all the player has to do is to spend it. It was not always like this, however. Take Sandy Lyle for example. Lyle was one of the great players of his generation, a golfer who won the British Open and the Masters but who, at the beginning, took far more interest in whacking a 2-iron off a hanging lie than he ever did looking after the checks that regularly drifted his way.

The alarm bells first rang for his manager, the redoubtable Derrick Pillage, when he took an urgent telephone call from Sandy's bank manager at his then hometown of Shrewsbury. The banker told a startled Pillage that he was a bit embarrassed to call but that he felt Mr. Lyle's financial advisor should know that there were many thousands of pounds lying in Lyle's current account and thus earning no interest.

Shortly after sorting this out Pillage had occasion to sift through his client's flightbag where he found cash and checks to the value of £3,000 and this in the days when £3,000 really was a significant amount of money. Says Pillage, "Sandy's explanation was that I had always told him to make sure he carried some cash around with him. I had to laugh."

remaining two players or he may stay by himself and play one against three (better ball). But any partner chosen must be selected BEFORE that player hits. However, if you decide to be the Lone Wolf then all stakes are doubled, each of the other three players betting two units, the Lone Wolf matching each for a total of six units. If there is a tie on a hole then, having previously decided, you may either call it quits and start again or carry the units forward to add to the next hole. Each player takes it in turn to be the Wolf. By the 16th hole this means you will have had four turns each and it is then the player who is losing most who is given the opportunity to be Wolf, Lone or otherwise, over the final two holes. Whether this is a good thing is debatable but that's how it is with a game that encourages much cunning.

VEGAS

HERE, without doubt, is a gambling game for people either with too much money or not enough sense. Personally, I wouldn't touch this game with your wallet, never mind mine, but the reason I've included it is for its curiosity value because this is one of the preferred games by the high rollers who inhabit Las Vegas. I suggest you read about it, digest it, and then forget it. Otherwise don't blame me if you lose the family home. Play Vegas, if you really must, during a four ball match. Divide into two teams and these sides then take the low score on their side and "attach" it to the high score. What? No, really it's simple. You and I are partners. You have a four while I score my usual six. This then is 46. Our opponents have two par fours so they have 44. Subtract their score from ours and we are two units down. What these units are worth is up to the participants as always. In Las Vegas this is unlikely to be less than $1,000. If someone shoots 10 or worse on any hole then the usual procedure is reversed so that instead of having, say, returned a team score that reads 510 it is reduced to 105. This is the good news; the bad stuff means that if your opponents have returned a 55 you are still 50 units adrift on this hole. Ouch! Or double ouch! You can see how this game really can hurt. Work it out from your scorecard next time your four ball has played and see how it would have worked out if you were playing for a dollar a unit. Then forget about it and get back to your usual Nassau game.

ODD-EVEN

QUICK, easy, and to the point, this game offers a bit of variety to your normal four ball match. I suggest you play it off the card when you have finished whatever your normal game is. As ever you align yourself with a partner and then all you need to do is to select which of you will return a score on the odd holes and which on the evens. These scores are then added up—or played out in a match-play format— to see who has won.

RABBIT

SIMILAR to the Snake game except in one vital regard. Whereas you want to get rid of the snake as soon as possible, you want to keep the rabbit for as long as you can. A player takes possession of the rabbit by winning a hole. The others then try to get it back. Or at least free it. This is done by someone else winning a hole outright. He doesn't then have the rabbit but he has freed it to run so that it is available for someone to win at subsequent holes. However, if the guy who holds the rabbit wins a second hole outright then he also gets a spare "leg" which means that two holes must be won by someone else just to set the rabbit running again. Yes, yes, it's crazy but it's also a bit of fun. Usually it is the person who has the rabbit after nine and then 18 holes that wins an agreed amount. And usually it is best to set the rabbit running again after those first nine holes rather than allowing the player in possession of the cuddly little thing to hold on to it.

MULLIGANS

A MULLIGAN is a shot that may be replayed and this can add a frisson of excitement to a match between two golfers of widely varying abilities. It's up to you and your opponent—or opponents, because the mulligan can be utilized well in a four ball game as well—how many mulligans a player may have. These will be on top of whatever strokes your handicap difference allows. The trick is to use the mulligan astutely. What exactly do I mean by this? Well, say you have missed a four-foot putt to win or halve a hole. Should you use a mulligan at this point or should you save it for when your drive scuttles into the water at the eighth hole, as it always does? It's up to you but, believe me, there are few things more galling than calling in a mulligan after missing that short putt and then going and missing the damn thing again.

Incidentally, who or what mulligan was originally is lost in the mists of time. Unless you know better, in which case please let me know. What I do know is that while a mulligan may save you money in a match, the pressure of knowing when to use the thing can cost a ditherer like myself dear.

STRING

FOR THIS game you each need a length of string and a knife. Please bear with me for this. My preference is for the string to be allocated according to handicap, to be precise 12 inches of string per stroke although this clearly can be varied. Anyway, armed with this length of string you may then use it to move your ball at any time by pulling out the string and marking to where you wish your ball to be moved. This length of string is then cut off. In this manner you may use a few feet to move away from a bush or tree and have a clear shot, or you may use just a few inches to get out of a divot.

DIABOLICAL FORTUNE

GOLFWRITER Derek Lawrenson was not playing for money when he took part in a special event involving the 1998 England football team. Instead this life-long Liverpool fan was just basking in the happiness he felt at partnering two footballers who were Liverpool stars at the time, Steve McManaman and Paul Ince. Perhaps the presence of this duo helped to focus Lawrenson more than usual on this day although as a long-time single figure handicap player he clearly has ability.

One of the short holes offered a truly glittering prize for a hole in one, a Lamborghini Diablo sports car worth a king's ransom. Lawrenson struck a three iron off the tee and then watched in a state of shock as his ball bounced a couple of times before dropping into the hole to secure this enviable prize. Asked if he was going to accept the car, and thus break his amateur status by a factor of at least 400 to 1, Lawrenson understandably replied, "What do you think?"

After driving the car for a month back at home he sold it for a significant sum of money and suffered happily on as a "non-amateur," which effectively meant that he could not represent his club nor play in, for example, the county team. This, he felt, was no real hardship. Incidentally, the maximum value of any prize for an amateur is now £500 in the UK, or $750 in the States. Or, if you're lucky, one tire on a Lamborghini.

You cannot use the string to hole a putt and you cannot use it to "re-cover" a lost ball. Unless you can see, and lift, the ball the normal lost ball rule is used. You may, however, use the string to move out of a hazard. Oh, and don't think that someone like, say, a two-handicap player is hugely disadvantaged by this string thing because the more accomplished the golfer, the better he can use moving his ball even an inch and into a perfect lie. Be warned.

FAIRWAYS & GREENS

HERE players pick up a point for each fairway hit in regulation on par 4s and 5s and one for each green hit in regulation. These points can be allocated every time a player hits the fairway or green or, if more than one manages it, the points available can be carried over to the next hole. It is completely up to you how you want to work it.

The (slightly) serious side to this particular game is that it encourages everyone to use smart play so that, instead of instinctively reaching for the driver, a golfer can take another club that gives him a better chance of actually hitting the fairway. This can prove more than a little helpful in aiding this player to reduce his handicap. On the other hand it may turn him into the dullest golfer in his crowd, and one that no one ever wants to play with again! Sometimes in golf, as in life, doing the smart thing, maybe even the correct thing, is not the best way to go.

YARDAGES

AWARD a point per yard of any hole won. Immediately you will realize that par 5s are the victories of choice in this rumble. If a hole is halved then no one gets the yardage unless you decide beforehand to split this yardage. At the end of the round add up the yardages of all holes won and allocate them to that player. How much should you play for? Not a lot really. Certainly no more than five cents. It's not uncommon for one player to have a winning yardage of around 2,500 yards, which the others then subtract their totals from and pay accordingly. The biggest loser may well be someone who has accumulated only 500 yards and so he owes the champ five cents x 2,000, which equates to $100. Better still, make it a penny a yard. Distance, sometimes, really does not lend enchantment.

BOBBY JONES

NAMED after the great man himself because of the instructional film he recorded when he was, by some distance, the most famous golfer in the world after winning the U.S. and British Amateurs and the U.S. and British Opens in 1930, a feat that we may say with some great certainty will never be repeated again. In the film, restored and reproduced on video, he is challenged by a member of the Riviera Club, in Los Angeles, to a match with no strokes involved. The catch was that Jones had to play his opponent's drives and vice versa. Each player, of course, must try his best off every tee otherwise there is no point. This is an interesting game for players of different abilities. It adds intrigue for both players, but it must be entered into in the right spirit and should be played off the back, or nearly back, tees.

SIDEBETS

SIDEBETS do what it says on the tin: they are bets embroidered around the main wager and must be decided before any game begins. Two of the most popular are Oozlems and Ferrets (incorporating the Golden Ferret).

OOZLEMS

THE OOZLEM is played for a unit stake wagered by each golfer in a two, three, or four ball match. The battleground is a par 3 hole. Say you are playing for $1 Oozlems. After each player has hit his shot into the green, whoever is closest (he must be on the green and if no one manages this then the next short hole becomes a double Oozlem) has the Oozlem honor and he must achieve par or better on the hole to win $1 off each of his partners. I recommend you also play reverse Oozlems, which means that if the player closest to the hole fails to get down in one or two more strokes then he pays each of his companions instead. This either ruins your putting forever or improves it no end.

FERRETS AND GOLDEN FERRETS

THE FERRET is played on a par 3 for an agreed unit stake as with the Oozlem. For this bet to activate, a player needs to hole a shot from off the green with any club but the putter. So it could be a chip-in from the fringe or a holed 5-iron from way back up the fairway. For the rarely seen Golden Ferret to raise its pretty head a player must be in a green-side bunker and must then hole his sand shot. There are no penalties for failing. Such feats are not routinely achieved by most club golfers so these are bets that are perhaps best suited to regular golfing partners. Some groups play for more than a year at a time without anyone having to pay out on this bet. Sound familiar?

OTHER BETS

WHILE these side bets are among the most common, there are, inevitably, a host of other bets that may be used during the game of golf. Here, for your delectation, are just some of these but, as always, use your imagination and try to come up with some of your own games next time you play with pals. Each is played for a unit stake that should be agreed beforehand. These stakes are known as "bits" and it's advisable for someone to keep a running total of who is doing what to whom so that you can settle up in the clubhouse afterwards without needing to go to arbitration.

WELL DID YOU EVAH?

BIG money matches have always been part of the scene at Sunningdale Golf Club, a quintessentially English heathland club sited on the Surrey/Berkshire border. While not every member plays golf for a significant wager, more than a few do, and often the amounts involved have become the stuff of legend.

Some years ago I interviewed a local man, Bill Hopkins, who from the age of 12 (1941) boosted his earnings by working as a Sunningdale caddie. As such he was privy to many of the biggest money games ever played on English soil and he often benefitted if his player ended up on the winning side. Not everyone was hugely generous, however, as Bill told me...

"I caddied for Bing Crosby several times and always found him a very hard man to work for. One day in 1973 I saw him at the club and he asked me to caddie for him. I'd already arranged a round so I said I couldn't. Now, Crosby was a very good player and he never went out to play without practicing properly first, but on this occasion he had not brought any practice balls with him. I told him I had a bucket of balls I could lend him.

"When I got back in from my round I asked the caddie-master if Mr Crosby had left anything for me. He said "yes" and handed me back the balls. I asked if he had left anything else but he said "no," not a shilling, not a thank you. Crosby? Now he was a tight old sod."

MURPHIES

IF YOU are off the green you can call a Murphy, which is to say you are betting your playmates that you can get up and down in no more than two strokes.

ARNIES

THE GREAT man often made par, or a birdie, without touching a fairway and sometimes you too play the game at least a bit like Palmer so why not reward those energizing moments when you pull off an unlikely par without gracing the really short grass? It will come as no surprise to learn that in Europe an "Arnie" is known as a "Seve" after Seve Ballesteros, golf's other great escape artist.

BAMBIS

ACHIEVING par after first striking a live animal. Points are deducted if it is decided that you deliberately aimed at the poor unfortunate beast and even more if you happen to fatally wound it. This is unlikely to even come into play during what we might call "urban golf" but you never know when a pesky squirrel may cross your path.

I once played at a course in the suburbs of Manchester, England, when my companion flushed a 4-iron that then dropped a passing pigeon. It was curtains for the bird I'm afraid but the good news is my opponent got to play his shot again. Well, good news for him.

WOODIES

THIS IS a side bet that is not much use if you only play links golf because what we need for this one is a host of trees on most holes. Hit a tree—it must be a solid clunk, not just a rustle among the leaves—and then make par and you will pick up the money. Hit two trees and the bet is doubled. If they don't play this at Harbour Town then they should!

FLAGGIES

THIS involves whacking your tee shot to within a flagstick's distance of the cup. The bet is doubled or even tripled if you also manage to hit the stick in the process. Mind you, tradition demands that you then pay money out if you miss the putt.

BARNES WALLIS

NAMED after the great British engineer Sir Barnes Wallis, the man who designed the bouncing bomb that destroyed the Ruhr Dam in 1943. In golf his name lives on if anyone manages to successfully skip their ball across water of any type. Not, to my knowledge, played in Germany.

WETWIPES

MAKING PAR despite hitting a ball into the *agua*. You may add a small twist to this by agreeing beforehand that a ball that successfully achieves the Barnes Wallis effect also counts.

WATSONS

IN 1982 Tom Watson finally won the U.S. Open. This he did at Pebble Beach, defeating his great rival Jack Nicklaus by one shot, and the reason he did this was because he chipped in for a birdie 2 at the 17th from the most unlikely position in deep rough behind that hole. It was an outrageous act of piracy, and ever since anyone who chips in from rough—proper rough—is said to have achieved a "Watson" and should be rewarded appropriately.

TOURNAMENT
FORMATS

THE POINT of any game is competition and although one of the benefits of playing golf is that you may, in the various ways already described, fly solo, the real thrill comes from pitting your skills, however ragged, against one, two, three, or many dozens of other players in an actual tournament. Traditionally, the main golf club method of doing this is via the Monthly Medal. Here is the heartbeat of the game for many players. Here, too, is where handicaps are most accurately assessed, judged, and moved up or down. For the uninitiated, the club medal is a properly conducted stroke-play competition. This is to say that every stroke counts and that your handicap is then subtracted from the total of shots used to cover 18 holes. There is much satisfaction and pride to be gained from these competitions.

THE MEDAL

PLAY THIS if you will. And, indeed, if you can. I have, and it's fun, plus if you just stick your name down on its own on a start sheet then you will end up meeting other members. Some of them will even be rather nice, interesting people. I say this because cliques in clubs are a monstrous pest and if there ever is a 35th Rule of Golf then my preference would be to see it allow for cliquish members to be taken outside and severely chastised for what I consider one of the bigger breaches of the game's etiquette. That, and reserved parking spaces for captains. You may be beginning to see why I may not be the most naturally clubbable golfer in the world. Anyway, medal, or stroke-play, golf has its serious place toward the center of the game but really it is the form of golf most disliked by all but the most accomplished of players. As described earlier, match play and Stableford are the preferred competition formats for the vast majority of us. But if you must play medal golf then allow me to suggest an interesting twist to the natural laws of this form of golf. Strictly unofficial of course but great fun nonetheless..

THE CALLOWAY SYSTEM

I CAME across the Calloway System some 20 years ago and I have been promoting its attractions ever since. What this system does is to allow for those irritating lapses of concentration or just bad luck that can shred a medal-play card swifter than a silken sheet hung out to dry in a hurricane. If ever you have limped back into the bar to announce, "I played my best golf today apart from a couple of horrid holes," then Calloway should be the game for you. Under this format you are allowed to discard your worst holes depending on what gross score you return as per the table shown on the next page.

No handicaps are used under the Calloway System. Logically, the lower a handicap then the lower score a player will return and the fewer, if any, half or whole holes he may

PRISONER-OF-GOLF

SOME golfwriters achieve greatness, a few have greatness thrust upon them, but only one, as far as I am aware, hit the heights because he was captured by the Germans. This was the irascible Pat Ward-Thomas whose scribblings for The Guardian *illuminated many a dull day and night. Pat was great for many reasons, but it was in a German prisoner-of-war camp that he achieved his finest moment.*

Unsportingly shot down over Holland while flying home to England, he thought he had gotten away with it when a farmer offered him sanctuary. Unfortunately, while Pat slept the farmer tipped off the Germans. He was fast asleep when a soldier prodded him awake with a rifle barrel. Pat's response was typical: "For Christ's sake, can't you see what time it is? Come back in the morning, I'm very tired." Instead he was bundled off to a POW camp, the one immortalized by the building of an escape tunnel under cover of a wooden exercise horse. This true story was turned into a book and a movie after the war but at the time it annoyed Pat. While the other chaps were tunnel building, he was busy building a mini-golf course in the camp. Worse, the wooden horse was placed right in front of Pat's fourth green. He went to the British C.O. to complain. Pat was all for the escape but he failed to see why his approach to the fourth should be interfered with in the process. He was advised this was the rub of the green and to get on with. So Pat introduced a local rule allowing the ball to be placed sideways without penalty and the Great Escape attempt carried on.

CALLOWAY SYSTEM SCORING

Gross Score	Subtract
73 or less	Zero holes
73 to 75	½ hole
76 to 80	1 hole
81 to 85	1½ holes
86 to 90	2 holes
91 to 95	2½ holes
96 to 100	3 holes

And so on, continuing in half-hole increments for every five strokes.

subtract from his score. Say a two-handicap golfer returns a gross 73 then he subtracts nothing as per the above table and that remains his score for the day. Say another player returns 97. This golfer gets to take away his three worst holes, which may be an eight, and two sevens. Thus 97 minus 22 equals 75. Not good enough to win but it has gotten him close and adds some real excitement, drama, and interest to the day.

This system is particularly useful if a large number of golfers are playing in a competition, some of whom are, shall we say, unsure of their handicaps as is often the case during company or corporate days. The Calloway System is a fun way of leveling out any iffy handicaps. Bandits are disarmed at a stroke under this method of play. And often it is even more fun to allow any hole to be discarded except the last. Playing the 18th hole well is always a competition within the competition and many feel that the pressure of maintaining a decent score by holding it together up the last should not be taken out of the game. It's surely a compelling point.

THE PEORIA SYSTEM

THE PEORIA SYSTEM, like the Calloway System, is particularly appropriate to utilize in a tournament when, for whatever reason, handicaps are not available for all players. The organizer for this competition secretly selects six holes, which, sensibly, should be a mixture of par-3s, par-4s, and par-5s.

When the players finish the organizer should total the score of each for these six holes, multiply by three, and subtract the course par. This figure then becomes that player's Peoria handicap. Subtract this handicap figure from the player's gross score for the day and that is his competition score.

And, glory be, it works decently well. For example, if a player shoots 28 on his secret holes then this multiplied by three becomes 84. Subtract the course par, say 72, and his handicap is 12. If his gross is 90 then 90 minus 12 gives him a net score of 78.

DROP OUT AND FLAG

IN SOME competitions just completing 18 holes is almost certain to make you a winner. Of these formats my two personal favorites are Drop Out and Flag. In Drop Out, foursomes pit their abilities against par under the Scramble format (that is, everyone hits from the tee, then everyone plays from the position of the selected best ball until a ball is holed). No handicaps are involved. Teams start on the first hole and continue to play until they fail to make par or better on any hole. Of course using the Scramble format par or better is odds-on at each hole but sometimes, especially when you know you will lose this particular competition, the pressure of just keeping going can mess up even a scramble team. It is not unknown for a team to bogey the first hole and while this makes them an object for good-natured ridicule it also suggests that Get Out is best played as a competition within a normal scramble. If more than one team completes 18 holes without a bogey then their actual score dictates the Drop Out champions.

Flag adds a solo twist to this drop-out format. This is an individual player competition where each golfer receives a number of strokes. The method for allocating these strokes is not set in stone but usually it is the par for the course plus two-thirds of handicap. So on a par 72 course a 16-handicapper would receive 11 strokes and an overall stroke allowance of 83. He also receives a flag of some kind

GREAT SHOT! WHO HIT IT?

SOMETIMES the rules may be, shall we say, bent a little. Or a lot. This is not to encourage cheating but merely to acknowledge that some moments, outside serious competition, are so attractive that it behoves a player to take advantage even if it means ignoring the rules.

Such a moment arrived for me some years ago when I was playing the Crans sur Sierre course that clings on halfway up a Swiss alp. This was by way of a course inspection before the European Masters took place. Led by the Tournament Director, John Paramor, and accompanied by two other journalists, we set off on a course that was now closed to practicing professionals, the last dregs of whom were making their way off. Unusually, I hooked my opening drive, my ball spearing over the trees and landing under the branches of an umbrella pine. When I found it, I stood there with a 5-iron in my hand, wondering what I could do. At that moment a familiar voice said, "Beel, Beel, quick." A moment later Seve Ballesteros was beside me. He looked at me, winked, looked at my ball, smiled, took my 5-iron, and crunched a shot. My ball set off low to escape the branches, then rose vertically over the high trees dividing the two fairways before turning sharp left and heading off to the first green some 180 yards distant. My partners, unaware of this swift drama, bellowed their appreciation from the other side. "How the hell did you do that? It's a fantastic shot," was the critique. It was only after our round that I told them. It remains the greatest shot I never played.

—a small white flag with his name written on it is good—
and he must plant this flag on the spot where his ball has
finished after his 83rd shot.

> The player who makes the most yardage before running
> out of strokes is the winner. Under a two-thirds of
> handicap system this is usually before 18 holes have been
> completed but if it is not then he may either play on until
> his strokes are used or you may declare the winner as the
> player with the greater number of strokes remaining in his
> locker after a completed round.

SCRAMBLE

THIS IS a competition for a team of at least three, preferably four, players and always adds gaiety to any group golf
outing. Everyone swings off the tee and then the best drive
is chosen, the ball is marked, and everyone has a go from
this spot. This system is used until the ball is in the hole
and, as before, an added piquancy can be embroidered into
the scramble by stipulating beforehand that each player
must produce at least three nominated drives. It is usually
advisable to get these out of the way as soon as possible as
otherwise the weaker golfer will turn into even more of a
gibbering wreck than usual if he is left with six holes to go
and still has to come up with his three drives. Apart from the

fun involved, the joy of scramble golf is that it encourages a real feeling of team spirit even if the purity of this camaraderie can be threatened if not one of the four of you manages to hole a 6-foot birdie putt. It also encourages players to shrug off negativity and to go for broke on every shot. The result, while frequently hilariously pathetic, is that much of the fear endemic to the game is removed. The best way to encourage this freedom is to have the most reliable hitter play last each time, his abiding presence freeing up the others to look, grip, and swing with a freedom that is too often absent from all our games.

SHAMBLE

IF YOU FEEL that the Scramble format is too artificial for your liking (and bears no relationship to your own usual game) then try Shamble. In this variation everyone tees off and then a best ball is selected and everybody plays from this spot. The difference from Scramble is that after this initial scramble each golfer plays his own ball from wherever it ends up. You may decide that each player plays his own ball on short holes from the tee—and I can understand why you would—but if you do then you may miss out on the delight of witnessing someone three-putt or, worse, while someone else in the same quartet holes out for a birdie two. A winning team can be decided on a "best two balls" basis or a high-low score or whatever method your imagination comes up with. Remember, the only rules to these unofficial competitions are the ones you decide on.

PINK BALL

PINK BALL is an increasingly popular game at those clubs that retain a sense of humor. Reassuringly, this is the majority. Whether it is a club or a society or a corporate day organizer who arranges Pink Ball, however, the result is the same—everybody is entertained. The basic game demands the use of, yes, a pink ball. Actually it can be any color as long as this color is distinctive to the extent that in no other circumstances would anyone wish to be caught using such a thing. The game is best used for four balls and goes as follows: Player One uses it on the first hole and it is then rotated around the rest of the team in strict order as play progresses at each subsequent hole. Those of you who are numerate will note almost immediately that as there are 18 holes to a round this means the first two players to use the ball will end up playing with it on holes 17 and 18 as well. Because of this the smart Pink Ball team will make sure that the better players use the ball on the first two holes. Whatever you decide, this pink ball score, whatever it is, must count toward two scores on each hole. If the pink ball golfer takes a double bogey and two teammates each enjoy a birdie then hard luck. One birdie counts, of course, but the Pink Ball effort must be added to it for that hole. Some harsh schools decree that only one pink ball is allocated and if it is lost then that is the end of that team's pink ball score. Better, I think, to throw in some extra pink balls. You can, if you wish, allow teams to score in the normal "best two scores to count" manner as well, so that the Pink Ball contest is a contest within the contest. But this version, while kinder, is for wimps.

ECLECTIC

ECLECTIC golf allows those of us who struggle to produce anything other than the seriously mediocre to briefly reach up and to touch the face of gods. Eclectic competitions are run over a period of time, perhaps winter, and require a number of stroke-play cards to be returned to an organizer. There may be a limit on the number of cards returned while some organizers require a small entrance fee for each card put in. At the end of the agreed time these cards are sifted through and the lowest score for each hole is noted.

This may mean over the course of a few months that a player who struggles to beat 90 most days returns an eclectic score in the 60s or even lower. In this way do we brush alongside the greats. A little bit.

ROUND ROBINS

ROUND ROBINS can be terribly frustrating both to organize and then to have arrive at some decent conclusion. Their merit lies in the fact that everyone tries to play everyone else (match play) in a club and so introductions are made and friendships begun between players who otherwise

WHAT A BRICK...

ALWAYS check the number of clubs in your bag. Or someone else's if you are caddying as I once did for Nick Faldo. I carried for the superstar as part of a charity round at Wentworth. It was a great day, raising several thousands of pounds for the Great Ormond Street Children's Hospital.

Everyone was happy when the 18 holes were completed, including me. But also I was tired. Lugging a pro bag across the demanding acres that make up the famed West Course in Surrey, England, was not easy.

To be fair, Faldo noted my discomfort and asked if I'd fancy being a full-time caddie for him. I declined the offer, explaining that I did not feel I had the necessary stamina to do such a job. He grinned. And so did the hackers who had paid a lot of money to join us for this special round.

Clearly, they knew something I didn't. "Count the clubs," advised Nick. I did. There were 17. "Now look in the bag," he further counseled. I did. There I discovered two dozen golf balls, two pairs of shoes and, right at the bottom, the biggest house brick Faldo could find.

That bag on that day almost literally weighed a ton. No wonder I felt tired. I've still got the brick. It's in my study. Faldo signed it for me after writing a short message that reads: "To Bill, what a BRICK!" At least I think it says BRICK.

may only have nodded at each other from time to time. The winner is the player with most victories but the problem with Round Robins is that it can be so difficult for players to actually meet the timetable. Because of this, provision has to be made for concessions and the problem then is that the winner may be the player who has profited from the most of these concessions. Still, it's worth a try if only from a social perspective.

PRO-AMS

THE WONDERFUL thing about pro-ams is that they allow us hackers to play with the best professionals in the world, although usually there is a handicap maximum (for men) of 18. The less than wonderful thing about these hybrid competitions is that quite often there are MEMBERS OF THE PUBLIC standing around snorting with derision at our amateur efforts. There is, however, an upside to this for I have found that I play some of what passes as my better golf in pro-ams and the reason for this is simple—I actually tend to concentrate properly in my desperation not to make a total, gibbering idiot of myself. The world will always be divided into those who do not mind performing in public and those who cringe pathetically at such a prospect.

Whichever camp you fall into I strongly urge you to take up any opportunity you ever have to play in a pro-am. The majority of professionals are politely attentive and quite often they are eager to help both your game and your understanding of pro golf by telling you tales about famous players that should never be repeated. At least not until you meet a few buddies. On top of this the course on which a pro-am is played usually has been carefully prepared and you will experience what it is like to putt on a fast surface. Plus the prizes are often significantly superior as well.

THE CHAPMAN SYSTEM

AND, FINALLY, a tournament format that allows men and women to play together and to have fun (well that is the aim at least). This is called the Chapman System and is named after its inventor, Dick Chapman, who was one of the very finest amateurs ever to grace the American golf scene.

Naturally he won the Amateur Championship during his long reign at the top of the nonpaid game but it is his amazing record of appearances in the Masters that not only defies belief but is a record that will stand in stone for all time.

In total he played 19 times at Augusta, a roll call of honors that contains another record that will never be beaten—by an amateur—for during this glittering sequence Chapman made 17 consecutive appearances.

He came up with his idea of a game for mixed pairs of varying abilities while practicing for Augusta at nearby Pinehurst. His wife often joined him on these trips and she wanted to play too.

Under the Chapman System both genders hit drives but then the man hits the woman's drive and vice versa. From this point they choose a "best ball" and play alternate shot golf until the hole is completed. It is generally accepted that three-quarters of the mixed pair's average handicap is the sensible thing to do. And the organizer may introduce a keener note into proceedings by specifying that each player must have at least half a dozen of their second shots chosen as "best ball" during the round.

I have found this a charming alternative to the usual mixed foursomes format—also known as "mixed gruesomes." As a growing number of women take up the game it is important that the genders should mix in a playing sense as well as at the bar. What is unfortunate is that women still play off their own, forward, tees. I say unfortunate because this inevitably leads to an irritating gap between the sexes, particularly if there is only one woman in a three or four ball match and she constantly is the last to hit no matter what her score was on the previous hole.

I have long campaigned for a "neutral" tee from which men and women may play at the same time with a sensible stroke reduction for men and a few strokes added for women. Why should I want this so much? Because the social aspect of golf is vital. Okay, if it is an important

PENNY WISE

SEVE Ballesteros has always been careful with money. His spirit is generous but he has a fine idea of how important money is and the need to nurture one's wallet. Certainly this was true during his early days on the European Tour when memories of a childhood that was hardly bathed in privilege were still vivid in his brain.

For much of his career Ballesteros went through caddies the way other men went through socks. His intensity and ambition, and his constant refusal to accept second-best, eventually made him a world champion but these are difficult qualities to walk alongside if you are the man carrying the bag and relating the yardages.

For a brief period in the early 1980s his caddy was Pete Coleman—later to strike up a successful partnership with Bernhard Langer—who was the first caddie to buy a Porsche. Coleman still laughs when he reflects on his experiences with the great man.

In those days there were no practice range balls and players had to supply their own. Caddies had to stand at the far end of the range and retrieve the balls while trying hard not to be brained by one. In Switzerland once Coleman carried out this duty all week and when the tournament was over he turned to Seve for payment but what was in his hand seemed short by quite a few dollars.

Coleman queried the amount, then Seve looked at him seriously and said, "At the start of the week I had 50 practice balls but now there are fewer than 40. I've charged you for the missing balls."

tournament we all may try to pull on our game faces as Tiger Woods does so often but, for us, golf should be about a convivial and entertaining few hours spent in company with the competitive element adding a sporting point to it all but never overriding the solitary fact that we are out there swinging clubs because it is a soothing antidote to the other irritants that embroider our modern lives. Well, it's a thought.

ETIQUETTE

IN common with all other games golf, obviously, is governed by a set of rules. Unlike the others, however, golf is also embellished seriously with the concept of etiquette. Now this does not refer to the correct manner by which to hold one's knife and fork when tackling the steak and scalloped potatoes that is the club chef's specialty. Neither does it cover the accepted way by which you may address the vicar and the lady captain if you discover them embracing behind the greenkeeper's shed (naturally, by now, you will know that you may drop them to the side without penalty). No, while the word etiquette is so old-fashioned that it throws up an image of discreet behavior at the Palace of Versailles in mid-18th century France, it is in fact much more important than mere social mores pertinent to the time. The dictionary defines etiquette in the context in which golfers need to use it: a conventional code of practice followed by certain groups.

The importance of this in golf cannot be overemphasized even if it can sometimes be used as a rather crusty old stick, which some older golfers may take to beat young upstarts about the head. Properly used, however, the observance of etiquette makes the game more enjoyable. And the latest revision of the rules—a task undertaken by the Royal & Ancient Golf Club of St. Andrews and the United States

Golf Association every four years—lays greater importance than ever on it.

For the first time a really serious breach of etiquette can lead to the culprit being disqualified. From the Monthly Medal to The Open Championship and with everything else in between.

This may appear a draconian reaction by the ruling bodies but it has come about because, as golf has spread around the world, there has been a tendency for too many new addicts to miss out on the spirit of the game. In the past new players have been coached gently by older ones on the etiquette of the game.

For the most part this has been easy to do because the overwhelming majority of new golfers have had to join a club to start playing the game. In this way the old, important flame has been passed on. Now, however, there are many millions of golfers who never join a club. Many behave well but some don't.

You will always come across the odd bad apple whose behavior leaves something to be desired. That's life I suppose but the fact remains that those golfers who shrug aside any real notion of etiquette—either because they regard it as something fusty that needs to be kept in a drawer somewhere or because they simply do not understand the concept—miss out on a core reason for playing golf in the first place.

THE SPIRIT OF THE GAME

ALMOST uniquely, the Powers That Be even define what exactly they regard as The Spirit of The Game under The Rules of Golf in their excellent handbook, and this is worth repeating here: "Unlike many sports, golf is played, for the most part, without the supervision of a referee or umpire. The game relies on the integrity of the individual to show consideration for other players and to abide by the Rules. All players should conduct themselves in a disciplined manner, demonstrating courtesy and sportsmanship at all times, irrespective of how competitive they may be. This is the spirit of the game."

So what does this mean? Well, like much else in golf, it is no more than a sporting extension of what we should all be doing in life generally. Stopping your car to allow someone to cross the road safely or holding a door open after you've passed through it to ease the passage of the person following are examples of what I call The Spirit of Life. It's the same in golf. Do unto others as you would be done to yourself. Golf, never mind life, is hard enough without trying to turn it into some sort of primeval struggle for survival.

Of course, within this context, the game should be played as hard as possible and with some wit. Laughing at an old friend's calamitous misfortune is perfectly permissible; but doing so with a new partner is not. Unless he starts laughing first.

GET ORRFF!

GOLF club secretaries used to be a unique breed. More often than not ex-servicemen, they continued to run clubs as a military camp. These were not men to trifle with. They had spent most of their adult lives with a Rule Book to guide them. No matter what the situation there always seemed to be a right or a wrong way of acting or reacting. The Book said so and they rarely, if ever, argued with The Book.

Perhaps their greatest champion was Paddy Hamner, who for years ran Muirfield. He was by nature irascible—although I have personal experience of his kindness—and his proudest boast was that no title or reputation ever impressed him. No matter who you were, if Paddy didn't like the cut of your jib then you didn't play his great links.

The story goes that one day a well-spoken man politely asked if he might have a game. Hamner looked at him and asked what school he had been to? "Eton," came the reply. "University?" "Oxford." "Were you in the services ever?" "Brigade of Guards, sir." "And your handicap?" "Scratch at present." "Very well, you may play nine holes," he harrumphed before stomping back into the clubhouse.

Some years later Paddy reached another level when he threw Tom Watson off the course for playing at night, his efforts illuminated by car headlights. Watson had just won the Open and was in celebratory mood but Hamner saw it differently and chastised the new champ. Actually, I suspect the old boy chuckled —to himself—all the way back to his bed.

SAFETY FIRST

IT IS NOT just manners, however, that we are focusing on here. Safety, too, is an important issue on a golf course. Hand a group of people some sturdy metal objects, some hard spheroid objects, and the capacity to bludgeon away and very swiftly someone can end up being seriously hurt. So always be aware of where your companions are standing before you take a swing, practice or otherwise.

Wait until the group of golfers in front is safely out of range before hitting your ball. Never work on the premise that you are unlikely to reach them unless you hit the ball as well as you once did a decade earlier on a bright, sunlit morning. Inevitably, Murphy's Law will kick in at times like these, and you will drive into them and your round—and theirs—may well be spoiled irretrievably.

Always alert green staff who may be working nearby or up ahead that you are about to hit a ball and if you do accidentally hit a ball in the direction of other players or staff then immediately yell a warning.

By tradition this is "FORE" and though any sort of shout is better than none at all the use of the word "fore" will immediately alert others that they may be in danger of a rogue ball landing on their heads. Remember to bellow at this point for a muted, perhaps embarrassed, shout is of no use. Stage whispers should be kept for theaters, not real-life dramas.

NOISE ON THE COURSE

OTHER THAN on the occasions outlined above the noise levels should be kept down. This is not to say that golf should be played in a sepulchral whisper. Just be reasonable and if there is a tee or a green close by where you are playing try to be aware of the other groups playing. The latest etiquette advice suggests that "any electronic device taken onto the course should not distract other players". This is unusually woolly advice from the Powers That Be. As far as many of us are concerned, electronic devices should never come on to a course. Almost the whole point of many rounds of golf is to get away from telephones and fax machines and the other clutter of modern life. If you must take your mobile phone out on a course with you then play with somebody else because I don't want your company, thanks. I do, however, make an exception for heart pacemakers—probably.

PACE OF PLAY

THE ACTUAL pace of play is vital. Only a thunderstorm can ruin a round of golf more than getting stuck behind an insensitively slow group who persist in stalking each shot, and particularly each putt, as though their lives depended on the outcome. The fact is that it is an individual's duty to keep up a decent pace. Simple things help here like assessing your shot while a companion is playing his so that within 30 seconds of his ball landing yours is on its way. Nowhere is this more important than on the green. Also if you are using a pull cart to carry your clubs then think about where you are parking it around the green. Spot where the next tee is and leave your cart between the green you are playing and this point. Never leave it at the front where you have just played a chip shot. It adds at least a couple of minutes to the playing of any hole and over a round this can add up to an unnecessary half an hour. Unacceptable. And fairly stupid.

It is pace of player, not numerical numbers, that dictates who has priority on a course. If you are in a two or three ball and the four ball behind are pressing you then allow them to pass at the first convenient moment. They may either be superior and swifter players or they may be playing foursomes, which is the quickest form of play of all. If you are beginning a search for a lost ball then do not wait until the legal five-minute hunt is up before calling the group behind through; call them through immediately and continue searching while they play the hole, remembering not to interfere with their actual game by causing a distraction as they play their second shots. Above all, do not call a group through and then, in the mistaken belief that you are adding to the pace of play, proceed to play your second shot to the green. This is even more annoying than being kept waiting on the tee, and actually slows them and almost always ruins that particular hole for everyone.

CARE FOR THE COURSE

UNDER ETIQUETTE, everyone has a duty of care for the course they are playing. In effect we all are part-time greenkeepers. Divots should be replaced; old divots that have been moved by a hungry bird in search of a worm should also be returned to their original spot. Bunkers should be raked properly before you leave and if someone earlier has failed to smooth out his footmarks then take care of that as well. Repair pitchmarks on the green. Not only the one you've just made but any others you can spot. Fix yours and someone else's is good advice to carry through your golfing life.

Do not drop the flagstick on the green as this can cause damage and try not to lean on your putter when picking your ball out of the hole. Never use a club to retrieve the ball from the hole as this can seriously damage it. If you must wear spikes—and the club allows them—then do not drag your feet on the green. Tap down any spike marks you see as you exit the green. This is a courtesy to the players behind.

If you are attending the flagstick for another player then ease it out of its socket before he actually putts as few things in life are more embarrassing than trying desperately to tug the damn thing out as his ball approaches. Remember that if you fail to remove it and his ball strikes it then he is penalized, not you, and such an incident will seriously test your relationship. Stand at arm's length from the flagstick to

KINDLY LEAVE THE CLUB

SOME golf clubs should come with a health warning. Certainly a man may find himself thrown out of a club for what appears to be the smallest of indiscretions. Such a club is Augusta National and such a man is Gary McCord, whose high reputation as a golf commentator has been built on an entertaining and colorful use of the English language. It was this talent that led to McCord being banned from covering the Masters or even entering the grounds.

This came after he described the Masters venue's legendary, quick greens as "so slick they might have been bikini-waxed." Unfortunately for McCord, Linda Watson, then married to Masters champion Tom, was listening at the time and expressed her distaste to her husband. He then wrote to the club to complain. This may read like an awfully small storm in a teacup but it was enough for the hapless McCord to find himself persona non grata which, as far as I know, he still is. Be warned. Careless talk can cost livelihoods.

This general rule at Augusta has now been expanded to include a ban on mobile phones, which even the Press have to keep in the Media Center. In 2005 a confused BBC radio reporter wandered outside for a breath of fresh air. Immediately a sharp-eyed security guy spotted the bulge in his pocket. Was it a mobile or was he just happy to be in Augusta? Both actually. The reporter was thrown out—even though the phone was switched off—and only high-level calls from London got him back in some hours later.

avoid treading on the ground too close to the hole, and if it is windy then hold the actual flag around the stick so that it does not flap. Oh, and be aware of where your shadow is falling. It is not helpful to have it thrown across the line of anyone's putt.

To the uninitiated all this etiquette stuff may appear to hold all the attraction of finding yourself in the middle of a minefield with the added complication of a blindfold. It is not. All this advice is, at root, no more than good sense on top of a consideration for others. It does, however, add hugely to the enjoyment of the game as well as helping to preserve the condition of the course. Until now the need for proper conduct on the course was, to a large extent, an optional extra. No longer is this the case. Consistently ignoring even the finer points of etiquette now may carry a penalty as severe as any in the game. In the latest Rules Book etiquette section the Powers That Be conclude that it is up to a club committee—or the majority of members if you are in a society—to take action for any persistent abuse of etiquette. They suggest that appropriate disciplinary action may include the suspension from play for a limited period of time or, in extreme cases, disqualification. We have yet to have the first golfer to be expelled from his club for serious breaches of etiquette but there will be one before long. Inevitably this will be interpreted in some quarters as just one more example of a game lost irretrievably in a pretentious, outmoded era. Not for the first time, such critics will be wrong. Golfers have a duty to respect the game, the course they are playing, and the person(s) they are competing against. Call me old-fashioned if you must but this philosophy seems to me to be the way forward not just for golf but for every game. It is golf's great strength that such values are now not just advised but, in effect, have become obligatory. Show me a reasonably mannered society and I'll show you a reasonably civilized one.

HANDICAPS

There are many things about the game of golf that set it apart from other sports, but perhaps the most profound of all is the unique and effective system of handicapping. This is what enables the young and the old, men and women, experts and hackers to tee it up together and enjoy a genuinely competitive game. You might be putting for bogies more often than birdies, but as long as you've got a realistic handicap, those bogies can put you within a hair of beating your club pro (or losing to the most hopeless beginner).

The essence of handicapping is that you are given a number of extra shots (over and above par) during the course of your round so that, if you play to your ability, when these shots are subtracted from your overall score, the result will be the par of the course. Therefore if you receive one of these shots at a par 4 and you take 5 to play the hole, you record a "net" 4. In medal play you take your extra shots according to the Stroke Index of the course, so if you have a 12 handicap, you receive a shot at Stroke Index 1–12. If you have a 23 handicap, then you receive two strokes at Stroke Index 1–5 and one at every other hole.

If you are playing match play it is the difference between handicaps that is used. These strokes are again taken according to the Stroke Index or Rating of each hole on the course. If one of you plays off 15 and the other off 22, then the difference is 7 and the higher handicap player receives his extra shots on the holes with Stroke Index 1–7.

CALCULATING HANDICAPS

Everyone has a basic playing handicap, but it's not always quite as simple as taking your extra shots at the right holes—the type of competition determines the number of shots that a player will give or receive during a competition, which may be a percentage of your full handicap. In the States, the U.S. Golf Association oversees the handicapping system. Handicap allowances have no effect in determining a USGA Handicap Index, however their use is recommended to produce fair competition. To make proper use of Handicap allowances, players first determine the Course Handicap then apply the handicap allowances for the appropriate format. If the percentage of a player's Course Handicap results in a decimal the figure is rounded off to the nearest whole number.

MATCH PLAY

Singles: The higher-handicapped player receives the full difference between the Course Handicap of the two players; the lower-handicapped plays from scratch.

Foursomes: The allowance for the higher-handicapped side is 50 percent of the difference between the combined Course Handicap of the members of each side. The lower-handicapped side competes at scratch.

Four Ball: The Course Handicaps of all four players are reduced by the Course Handicap of the player with the lowest handicap, who plays from scratch. Each of the other players is allowed 100 percent of the difference.

If a match goes into a sudden-death playoff then strokes continue to be taken on the extra holes according to the Stroke Index of the course.

STROKE PLAY

Singles: Each competitor receives his full Course Handicap.

Four Ball: Men receive 90 percent of Course Handicap; Women receive 95 percent of Course Handicap.

Foursomes: The allowance is 50 percent of the partners' combined Course Handicap.

Stableford Singles: Players use full Course Handicap, and strokes as they are allocated on the scorecard.

DIFFERENCE CALCULATIONS

If you're not up to higher mathematics on the first tee, the table on the next page gives a quick reference for calculating handicap differences based on ¾ and ½ handicaps as well as $^7/_8$ and $^3/_8$, which are also sometimes used.

DIFFERENCE	7/8	3/4	1/2	3/8
1	1	1	1	0
2	2	2	1	1
3	3	2	2	1
4	4	3	2	2
5	4	4	3	2
6	5	5	3	2
7	6	5	4	3
8	7	6	4	3
9	8	7	5	3
10	9	8	5	4
11	10	8	6	4
12	11	9	6	5
13	11	10	7	5
14	12	11	7	5
15	13	11	8	6
16	14	12	8	6
17	15	13	9	6
18	16	14	9	7

DIFFERENCE	7/8	3/4	1/2	3/8
19	17	14	10	7
20	18	15	10	8
21	18	16	11	8
22	19	17	11	8
23	20	17	12	9
24	21	18	12	9
25	22	19	13	9
26	23	20	13	10
27	24	20	14	10
28	25	21	14	11
29	25	22	15	11
30	26	23	15	11
31	27	23	16	12
32	28	24	16	12
33	29	25	17	12
34	30	26	17	13
35	31	26	18	13
36	32	27	18	14

GOLFER'S GLOSSARY

A

Ace: A hole-in-one.

Address: Position taken by a player prior to hitting a shot.

Albatross: A double eagle; a score of 3 under par on a hole.

Apron: The closely mown fringe of a putting green.

B

Back Nine: The final nine holes of an 18-hole round.

Birdie: A score of 1 stroke less than par on a given hole.

Bisque: A handicap stroke, which a player can elect to take at any time during a match.

Bogey: A score of 1 over par on a hole.

Borrow: A term referring to how much a ball will turn or break when putted.

Break: The amount of curve of a putt as it rolls.

Bunker: A type of hazard, usually a well or depression filled with sand or bare earth.

C

Casual Water: Temporary accumulation of water on the course that is visible before or after the player takes his stance.

Chip: A short shot, often played to the green with a higher lofted club.

Chunk: A chip resulting in more turf being removed than desired. May also be called a "chili dip".

Cut: A shot, slicing or fading the ball and causing it to move from left to right (for the right hander).

D

Divot: Turf removed from the ground when playing a shot.

Dogleg: A golf hole with a marked change of direction in the fairway, usually designed to restrict the drive.

Dormie: In match play when a player is the same number of holes "up" as there are holes left to play and therefore can no longer lose.

Double Bogey: A score of 2 over par on a hole.

Double-Eagle: A score of 3 under par on a hole, also called an albatross.

Draw: A shot that curves from right to left in the air (for the right hander).

Drive: The first shot on a hole, played from the teeing ground.

Dropping Zone: An area in which a player may drop his ball under penalty of one stroke, usually available where it is not practical to follow the usual procedure for relief from a hazard.

Duck Hook: A shot that begins straight and then curves uncontrollably from right to left (for the right hander).

E

Eagle: A score of 2 under par on a hole.

Even Par: A player's score that matches the par for the course at any point during a round.

Explosion: A type of shot, typically played out of sand.

F

Fade: Intentional shot that curves gently from right to left (for a right-handed player).

Fairway: Closely mown area of the course between tee and green.

Fat: Hitting the ground slightly before the ball and thus dramatically reducing the distance hit.

First Cut: Term given to a section of "semirough" bordering a fairway.

Flagstick: Marker indicating the position of a hole.

Flyer: An unexpectedly long shot caused by grass being trapped between the ball and the clubface and reducing spin.

Fore: The word shouted to warn other golfers of danger.

Four Ball: A match in which two players play their better ball against the better ball of two other players.

Foursome: A match in which two players play against two others, with each side playing one ball.

Fringe: Area of grass that borders a putting green.

Front Nine: The first nine holes of an 18-hole golf course.

G

Gimme: A putt conceded to a player without his having to play it; usually so short that it would almost certainly be holed.

Grain: Direction of growth of grass on a green, which can affect the run of the ball.

Green Fee: Fee charged to play a golf course.

Greensome: A variation of foursomes golf in which both partners drive at every hole then choose one of their balls with which to complete the hole.

Ground Under Repair (GUR): A marked area of the course from which a player is entitled to remove his ball and drop clear without penalty.

H

Half: A shared hole in match play; the result of opponents returning the same net score on that hole.

Hanging Lie: A ball resting awkwardly on a slope.

Hazard: A bunker or water hazard as defined by the committee.

Heel: The part of the club head closest to the shaft.

Home Green: The last hole to be played on a golf course.

Hook: A shot that curves, usually uncontrollably, from right to left (for a right hander).

Hosel: The neck of an iron club head into which the shaft is fitted.

K

Knock-Down: Shot intentionally played to keep a ball low in the wind, usually with a longer iron than would normally be required for that distance.

L

Lag: A long putt intended not to go in the hole but to leave as short a tap-in as possible.

Lie: Term used to describe the nature of a ball's position on the course during play.

Links: Properly a golf course built on linksland by the sea, but also loosely applied to a course of any description.

Lip: The edge of the hole.

Lip Out: A ball that rolls around the lip of the hole but fails to go in.

Local Rules: Additional rules applied by club committees to cover specific local conditions.

Loose Impediments: Natural objects on the golf course that are not fixed or growing.

M

Mashie: Archaic term for a lofted iron club roughly equivalent to a 5-iron.

Match Play: Form of play in which the score is kept by the number of holes won and lost.

Medal Play: Type of competition in which the lowest total score (number of strokes) wins. The same as stroke play.

Mulligan: An unofficial dispensation to replay a bad shot, most often applied on the first tee.

N

Nassau: A three-part bet on the front nine, the back nine and the overall game.

O

Out of Bounds (OB): Any area designated as such, often beyond the boundaries of the course, from which play is prohibited.

Outside Agency: The term used to describe something outside the match that interferes with it, such as a dog or a bird.

P

Par: The score a scratch player is expected to score on a given hole based on its length and difficulty.

Penalty: A stroke or strokes added to the score in accordance with the rules.

Pin high: A shot finishing level with the flagstick and therefore perfect for distance if not direction.

Pitch: Short approach shot to a green made with a lofted club.

Pot Bunker: A small but very deep bunker, usually filled with sand.

Preferred Lies: A local rule, commonly applied in the winter or during abnormally wet conditions, allowing a player whose ball lies on the fairway to pick it up, clean it and replace it before playing his shot.

Pro-am: A competition involving professional and amateur golfers.

Provisional Ball: A second ball played as a precaution when it is suspected that the first may turn out to be lost.

Pull: A shot that goes straight to the left of its target (for a right hander) without curving in the air.

Punch: A deliberately low shot played with a shortened swing.

Push: A shot that goes straight to the right of its target (for a right hander) without curving in the air.

Putting Green: The area of the hole being played that is specifically mowed for putting.

R

Relief: Placing or dropping a ball, with or without penalty depending on the situation, in order to be able to be able to make a normal stroke at it.

Rough: The coarser or longer grass or generally unprepared areas of a golf course bordering the fairways from which it is more difficult to play.

Rub of the Green: The occurrence of a ball being deflected or stopped by an outside agency. Also applied to any piece of good or bad luck for which there is not provision in the rules.

S

Sand Trap: Alternative term for a sand bunker.

Scratch: A handicap of zero.

Shank: A shot that is struck in the hosel area of the golf club resultingin the ball shooting out almost at right-angles.

Shotgun Start: When competitors all begin play simultaneously from different tees around the course, signalled by a shotgun.

Sky: A shot, usually caused by the ball missing the clubface of a wood and coming off its top causing the ball to travel high and drop short.

Skull: Striking the top of the ball and causing it to scuttle off low.

Slice: A shot that curves uncontrollably from left to right (for a right hander).

Slope (Index): A formula used to compare the difficulty of different courses.

Stableford: A scoring method allocating a number of points for the score made on each hole rather than counting every shot.

Stimp: The unit of measurement for the speed of a green.

Stimpmeter: Device used to measure the speed of a green, consisting of a ramp of a fixed height down which a ball is rolled. The distance the ball then rolls beyond it on a flat area of the green is given as the speed rating.

Stroke and Distance: Term used to describe the penalty when playing a second shot from the same spot (e.g. if a ball is hit out of bounds) – one stroke and the further penalty of the distance.

Stroke Play: Form of play, also called medal play, in which every stroke is counted and the lowest number taken wins.

Stymie: Archaic term referring to the situation where an opponent's ball lay between yours and the hole. Until a rule change in the early 1950s, it could not be moved.

T

Takeaway: The start of the backswing.

Tee (or teeing ground): The prepared area from which the first shot is taken on every hole. Also the wooden or plastic peg on which a ball is placed prior to the play of the first shot on a hole.

Tee Marker: Object marking the area from which a ball must be played at the beginning of each hole, usually colour-coded to provide different tees for varying abilities.

Three Ball Match: A match in which three players play against one another, each playing his own ball. Each player is therefore simultaneously playing two separate matches.

Threesome: A match in which one player plays against two, each team playing one ball.

Through the Green: The term covering everywhere on the course that is not the tee, the green or a hazard.

Toe: The outside end of the clubhead, furthest away from the shaft. Also the term applied to a shot played unintentionally from this part of the club.

Top: A shot striking the ball halfway up or above and causing it to shoot off low.

Turn: The halfway point of an 18-hole round, deriving from traditional courses such as St Andrews where the first nine holes are all out towards the furthest point on the course and the second nine work their way back to the town.

U

Up and Down: Holing out (from off the green) in two
   shots. One shot up and one putt down.

W

Waggle: Movement of the club away from and back to
   the ball to relieve tension before making a swing.

Water Hazard: Any area of a course so designated, usually
   containing water.

Winter Rules: Local rules applied to aid golfers and
   protect courses during the winter months, most
   commonly 'preferred lies'.

Y

Yardage Marker: Stakes at the edge of the fairway or discs
   sunk into the fairway giving the exact yardage to the
   front or centre of the green.

Yips: The psychological block that causes golfers to miss
   short putts.

INDEX